About

College Application Essays

Tamar Schreibman

SPARK
COLLEGE

AN IMPRINT OF SPARK PUBLISHING

WWW.SPARKCOLLEGE.COM

W9-BCK-632

Spark Publishing
A Division of Barnes & Noble
120 Fifth Avenue
New York, NY 10011
www.sparknotes.com

ISBN-13: 978-1-4114-0349-9
ISBN-10: 1-4114-0349-5

Library of Congress Cataloging-in-Publication Data available upon request.

Please submit changes or report errors to **www.sparknotes.com/errors**.

Printed and bound in Canada.

3 5 7 9 10 8 6 4

CONTENTS

Why 10 Things?

It seems like everyone's writing books that claim to give you the basics, nice and simple—but what you get are pages overstuffed with lots of information you just don't need.

With *10 Things You Gotta Know*, we give you *exactly* what you need—no more, no less. We know you want your knowledge *now*, without wasting time on information that's not important. Learning 10 quick basics is the way to go.

Each 10 *Things* book contains:

- Lots of clear headings for skimming
- Sound bites of text that are easy to digest
- Sidebars that enhance your understanding
- Tons of Top 10 Lists for vital facts at a glance

Sure—maybe you could argue that there are 8 vital things, or 11. This isn't rocket science. But 10 is such a nice, even number—and who doesn't love a great Top 10?

In this book, we focus on 10 things you gotta know about writing college application essays:

1. **The Point**

   There's no way out of it: if you're applying to college, you have to write the application essay. We explain how to use this opportunity as an advantage to craft the exact message you want to deliver.

2. **The Topic**

   Here you'll find all kinds of tips about what you should—and shouldn't—write about. We give you some actual sample prompts from the Common Application and from specific schools. We also help you get started and show you what to do when you get stuck.

3. **The Structure**

   Now that you know what you want to write about, you need to figure out how to write about it. This chapter explains a few different ways to build your essay and discusses each structure's strengths and weaknesses.

4. **The Rough Draft**

   It's time to put pen to paper (or fingers to keyboard) and start writing. Here we help you avoid procrastination, explain how to write a rough draft, and go over some sample drafts.

5. **Voice**

   How you sound in your essay is just as important as what you say. Your essay should showcase the real you—and here we show you how to avoid the 10 most common pitfalls and put the best you forward.

6. **Organization**

   Here, we review the building blocks of paragraphs and essays, including thesis statements, topic sentences, introductions, transitions, and conclusions.

7. **Standing Out**

   Your essay is your opportunity to differentiate yourself from other applicants and to show the admissions committee that you're more than a mishmash of test scores and grades. Telling stories and giving details are the keys to writing a lively, engaging essay.

8. **Grammar & Punctuation**

   While one comma splice won't destroy your chances of admission, several grammar errors will. This chapter reviews the 10 most common writing errors made in application essays and includes a crash-course grammar guide.

9. **The Final Edit**

   Good writing doesn't just happen: you need to write, rewrite, edit, and repeat as necessary. Here we go over some helpful strategies and give you two checklists to use before you send off your application.

10. **Real Essays**

    Want to see some essays that really worked? The essays in this section are smart, polished, and engaging—and helped get their authors into their top-choice schools.

Before we get started, take a look at these 10 questions to see how much you really know about writing a college application essay. The answers follow.

1   The secret to writing the college essay is:
   - **A.** To figure out what the admissions officers want to hear and then to say it.
   - **B.** To sound as well spoken and well read as any English teacher.
   - **C.** There is no secret. All I can do is try my hardest to write a thoughtful and honest essay.
   - **D.** To get it over with as quickly as possible so I can focus on enjoying senior year.

2   Finish the following sentence: I should start writing my college essay _____.
   - **A.** Tomorrow. I've been saying that for months now, but this time I really mean it. What? Did you say everyone's going to the beach tomorrow?
   - **B.** Years ago! I will never figure out what to write about and won't have enough time to make it perfect. Man, am I stressed out.
   - **C.** The night before the essay is due. I work best under pressure. Plus, how long can one of these things take?
   - **D.** Now. I'm the kind of person who likes to have plenty of time to come up with ideas, write many drafts, get feedback, and proofread a million times.

3   If you have tried and tried but can't figure out what to write about, you should:
   - **A.** Give up. You surely have nothing interesting or original to say.
   - **B.** Ask your mom to pick a topic for you.
   - **C.** Do some research. Ask your siblings, parents, or friends to list three adjectives that describe you and to share anecdotes that illustrate their point.
   - **D.** Reiterate your grades and activities in essay form.

4   **The structure of your essay:**
   A. Doesn't matter. The secret is finding the right topic and using as many impressive words as you can.
   B. Helps the reader think about your topic by framing your material.
   C. Must follow the exact rules you learned in ninth grade for structuring an essay.
   D. Isn't something you need to think about; just put the words on the paper in the order they come to you.

5   **You have chosen a topic, you know which anecdotes and key details you want to include, and you have selected a structure. Now you are ready to write a rough draft. You should:**
   A. Sit down in front of your computer and stare at the blank screen until the perfect first sentence springs into your head.
   B. Just start writing and start anywhere. Don't worry if it is any good. You can rework, revise, and polish later. The sooner you begin, the sooner you'll have a rough draft to work with and the more time you will have to make it better.
   C. Turn on the TV, check your email, play some Tetris, listen to your iPod, call a friend. You don't feel like writing now, so why should you push it?
   D. After you write each sentence, reread it to make sure it sounds good. If it isn't perfect, delete it and revise it until it is the paradigm of all senteces.

6   **Now that you've finished your rough draft, it's time to:**
   A. Catch up on all *The Sopranos* episodes you Tivo-ed when you were too busy working on your rough draft to watch TV.
   B. Proofread it and send it to all the colleges on your list.
   C. Reread it to see if your thesis is clear and whether all the points in your essay support your thesis.
   D. Party! You spent way too long on the rough draft. Now that the hard part is over, it's time to relax.

7 The voice you use in your essay should:
   A. Read like your speaking voice but more polished.
   B. Sound the way you imagine the admissions officers would like you to sound.
   C. Sound exactly the way you write when you email your best friend.
   D. Be true to whatever mood you were in when you wrote the rough draft.

8 If you want to convey happiness to your reader:
   A. Make sure you are in that mood when you write the essay.
   B. Think back to how you felt and describe it.
   C. You should say "I felt happy."
   D. None of the above.

9 Showing that you have a basic understanding of grammar:
   A. Is not important. Only English teachers care about that stuff. The colleges are more concerned with content.
   B. Is the sole purpose of the essay. One comma in the wrong place and you've blown your chances of getting into college.
   C. Illustrates that you take this process seriously and that you will be able to thrive academically in college.
   D. Is proof that you don't have a creative bone in your body.

10 When your reader comes back to you with suggestions, you should:
   A. Listen quietly, read over the notes, let the comments sink in, and then try to incorporate the ones that make sense to you.
   B. Incorporate each and every suggestion, no questions asked.
   C. Insist on concrete examples if you receive any negative feedback.
   D. None of the above.

Answers

1

Answer: C. Despite what you may have heard, there is no secret ingredient that will get you into the college of your choice. The goals in writing your application essay are to be honest and thoughtful and to write well. Be disciplined and true to yourself throughout the process, and your best qualities will shine through. **See Chapter 1.**

2

Answer: D. Writing is a process that takes time. Even if you have great ideas in your head, getting them down on paper can be a challenge. The more time you give yourself, the more opportunities you'll have to improve your essay. Start now! **See Chapter 2.**

3

Answer: C. Keep digging. It is helpful to bounce your ideas off a trusted relative, friend, or teacher, but don't let anyone else pick your topic for you. **See Chapter 2.**

4

Answer: B. With a personal essay, you have more freedom with structure than you do with an academic essay, but that doesn't mean you don't need one at all. Your structure will determine how your reader experiences your essay, so put some thought into which one will work best for your material. **See Chapter 3.**

5

Answer: B. The only way to write is to write. No matter how much thinking you do before you start to write, you aren't going to bang out the perfect essay the first time you try. Good essays do not flow out of your head, down your arm, into your fingers, and onto the page, whole and formed. **See Chapter 4.**

6

Answer: C. Be proud of yourself for finishing your rough draft. You are on the right track. But you still have more work ahead of you. **See Chapter 6.**

7

Answer: A. Your writing voice should sound like you when you're having your most inspired conversation. Remember that the people reading your essay have never met you before. You want to show them the best you. **See Chapter 5.**

8

Answer: B. Writing about something that is important to you is a basic tenet of writing. If you can connect emotionally to your topic, then you will be able to describe how you felt—rather than state it—in a way that resonates more with your reader. **See Chapter 7.**

9

Answer: C. An essay that is grammatically flawless does not guarantee admission. One typo probably isn't going to be a deal breaker, but you should strive for perfection. It will illustrate that you have a grasp of the English language and that you are a conscientious student. **See Chapter 8.**

10

Answer: A. It is only natural to feel defensive when someone suggests that you make changes to a piece of writing you've been working on for a long time. But remember that you chose this person for his or her intelligence and honesty. You don't need to take every single suggestion to heart, but, ultimately, feedback from a wise and thoughtful person will enhance your essay. **See Chapter 9.**

1
THE POINT

"What lies behind us and what lies before us are tiny matters compared to what lies within us."

Ralph Waldo Emerson

There are two reasons why colleges ask you to write an essay as part of your application:

1. To show the admissions committee who you are, in addition to what you've done.
2. To show the admissions committee you can write.

Revealing Yourself

By the time the people on the admissions committee get around to reading your essay, they already know about all the activities, AP classes, and accomplishments you have under your belt. What they really want to learn from the essay are things they can't figure out just by reading the rest of your application. Through the topic you choose, the details you include in your essay, and your voice and writing style, the admissions officers will learn a tremendous amount about your personality, your values, how you think, and what makes you tick. A 500-word limit won't give you space to reveal everything about yourself, but it will give you an opportunity to highlight a slice of who you are. You want that slice to be interesting and engaging.

"The essay gives the application a voice," says Margret Korzus, Associate Dean of Admissions at the University of Denver. "Everything in the essay comes to us secondhand. Courses and grades can't be changed; recommendations are how other people see you and evaluate you. The essay is truly the only part of the application, especially for colleges that don't do interviews, that allows you to tell us who you are."

The essay is the only part of the application over which you have total control. Use this to your advantage and craft the exact message you want to deliver.

Admissions officers have mountains of essays to read. Picture a harried admissions officer who has to present candidates from your region to the committee first thing in the morning. It's 2 A.M., and he's trying to burn through a stack of 200 essays. You have to help this admissions officer understand how special you are and why the committee should accept you. If the school has 6,932 other applicants, there's a good chance that among them there's another girl from another high school who also plays the piano, serves on the student council, and has a 3.8 GPA. This is your opportunity to distinguish yourself from her.

The Admissions Committee

Before we go any further, let's get to know your audience a little bit better. Do you imagine an admissions officer reading your essay with a red pen in her hand, frothing at the mouth in gleeful anticipation of finding mistakes so she can laugh maniacally at your expense and toss your file in the garbage? Or a group of crusty old men sitting with their arms folded over their chests, frowning and shaking their heads in disappointment?

Admissions Officers, Demystified

The truth is the admissions officers are just people. The difference between them and everybody else on this planet is they are trying to create the best first-year class possible—strong students who seem likely to graduate and will have a positive and fruitful experience at their school. They are looking for young people who will enrich the dynamics of campus life with their thoughts, passions, and personalities. They don't expect perfection. They are, after all, looking to fill the class with human beings.

At most schools, at least two admissions officers will read your essay. Each of these admissions officers has to read hundreds of essays—some as many as a thousand—and will spend an average of ten to twenty minutes reading yours.

After two officers read your essay, your application goes to the admissions committee, which usually consists of some combination of the following people: director of admissions; one or two senior officers, among them usually a regional reader who looks at all applications from a particular geographic area; a recent graduate; a member of the faculty; and a few current students.

Keeping It Real

Admissions officers are not all the same. Some are recent graduates, while others have been in the profession for thirty years. Some are a laugh-a-minute, while others are humorless. Some are sticklers for structure, while others are suckers for creativity. You get the idea. Attempting to target a particular reader is a waste of your time.

Write about what you want to write about, not what you think the admissions officers want you to write about. Your essay won't ring true if you don't focus on what's in your heart. When a writer is genuinely connected to a topic, the reader can tell and will want to keep reading. Don't worry if you don't think you have anything interesting to say. We promise that you do! We'll explore how to find the right topic in Chapter 2.

Writing Ability

Many jobs require writing skills, and employers will be looking for people who know how to communicate clearly. This is the reason why colleges are doubling their efforts to teach students to write. This is also why the new SAT has a writing section. Colleges need to know that you have basic writing abilities before they admit you. They want to see that you can organize your thoughts and argue persuasively. But your goal in writing your application essay is also to hold their interest and win them over with original thoughts. As one New York City English teacher put it, "The best self-advertisement is to write something worth reading."

Writing, Demystified

Writing isn't as scary as most people think. It's really just thinking on paper and then going back to organize and refine your ideas and language. It's not easy, but you can do it if you put in the time and effort.

With a personal essay, the first step is to make like Popeye and say to yourself, "I yam what I yam." So if you're a science whiz, don't waste your time despairing that you're not a poet (and don't try to pretend that you are one). If in the back of your mind you're kicking yourself for not having learned Swahili and taken up karate, you will end up wasting precious energy that you could otherwise have used to highlight an extraordinary quality that you do possess.

Timetable

Writing a personal essay is a demanding process. You should plan on spending considerably more time on this essay than you spent on the last English paper you wrote. In a perfect world, you would have spent the summer between your junior and senior years reading personal essays by famous authors, reflecting on the meaning of life, checking out essay questions on college websites, and maybe even working on a rough draft.

But let's be honest: over the summer you were hanging out at the beach with your friends, canoodling with your sweetheart, and working to save up some cash for college. Now, in between settling into your senior year, going to soccer practice, catching up with your friends who were away all August, figuring out whom you want to ask out, getting used to your classes, and narrowing down the list of schools you want to apply to, reality is slowly sinking in: it's time to start the essay. Luckily, you're reading this book. And our promise to you is: you still have time.

10 THINGS

Admissions Committees Want

1

Self-revelation

2

Honesty

3

Organization

4

Directness

5

Clarity

6

Concision

7

Candor

8

Sincerity

9

Originality

10

Good syntax

Feeling Overwhelmed?

The best way to handle a skyrocketing stress level is to break down the process and focus on small tasks. While you're brainstorming, don't think too much about the writing. While you're writing the first draft, don't look ahead at how much more you have to do. Don't beat yourself up for not being further along in the process. Each step is necessary: take them one at a time, and you will finish.

> "Mentally, fallow is as important as seedtime. Even bodies can be exhausted by over-cultivation."
>
> **George Bernard Shaw**

Ask for Help

When you are writing about yourself, getting someone else's perspective is especially important. Ask a friend, a relative, or a teacher to kick around some ideas with you and to read your first draft and give you feedback on it.

While your essay is in someone else's hands, avoid working on it or obsessing over it. "Even when you're not actively writing, your mind still works. By taking time off, you will be able to revise with better perspective than if you were to work on it every hour before it's due," says Kelly Tanabe, cofounder of SuperCollege.com.

Never Too Early to Start

If you're a junior and you are reading this, congratulate yourself for thinking ahead. The summer is a good time to start brainstorming and reflecting on your experiences and your qualities. In early July, most colleges will put their applications online so you can see what questions they ask, which gives you an opportunity to start focusing on specifics. You might want to carry the questions and a notebook with you to jot down ideas as they pop in your head.

10
BIGGEST
Essay Turnoffs

1

Boasting

2

Shameless flattery

3

Begging

4

Spelling errors

5

Clichés

6

Big, clunky words

7

Generalizations

8

Insincerity

9

Vagueness

10

Failed attempts at humor

2
THE TOPIC

"You always find things you didn't know you were going to say, and that is the adventure of writing."

John Updike

Chances are you're wondering, "What in the world should I write about?" You're not alone. Everybody who has ever had to write an essay for a college application has probably asked that very question. And the applications don't give you much guidance: most of the essay questions are so open-ended that you can write about virtually anything you want. Don't believe us? Take a look at pages 12–13.

Although picking a topic will seem daunting at first, it's not an impossible task. The key is to narrow your focus and write about something close to your heart. If you follow this plan, you'll create a lively essay that showcases your intelligence and personality to the admissions committee. But finding a great topic is not something you can do in five minutes. It will take a little work.

Starting

One of the most difficult parts about writing is the sense of dread and impending doom that haunts all writers before they actually sit down and start. That's why we recommend starting the process as early as possible. The sooner you start thinking and brainstorming, the less heinous the process will be. Once you start, you'll feel better, you'll realize how much potential material you have, and you'll have more time to let your creative juices flow.

Think, Think, Think

Early on—say, four or five months before applications are due—start thinking about possible topics. Go about your normal routine, but tuck the topic question in the back of your mind. Try to note what about the world you appreciate and are interested in. Carry a notebook to jot down thoughts. Give it time, and chances are you'll come up with some good stuff.

If you wait until the night before the application deadline to choose your topic, you'll find yourself staring at your computer screen in a cold sweat, frantically wondering whether you should write about your love of the rainforest, that time you stole second base in junior high, or maybe, um, what your bedroom's décor says about you. If you wait until the last minute, it is highly unlikely that your essay will be a thing of beauty and interest. These things take time.

Brainstorming

As you probably know from school, brainstorming is the process of getting ideas and thoughts down on paper. Brainstorming doesn't have to be logical or tidy; you can scribble down (or type) ideas in any way that makes sense to you. And don't worry about editing yourself as you brainstorm. No one is going to see this part of the process except you, so let the good ideas and the not-so-good ideas flow freely.

When you're brainstorming ideas for your college application essay, let your mind wander. Think about issues that matter to you, important moments in your life, high school experiences that stand out in your mind, and places and people that left an impression on you. Jot down emotions you often experience, verbs that mean something to you, and smells that bring back strong memories. Don't limit yourself to happy experiences—not all good stories are happy stories. Maybe one of your keenest memories is of sitting and crying on the steps outside the school auditorium after you found out you didn't make the varsity team. If a moment was meaningful to you and you can connect to your emotions while you write, your reader will connect to your story. The point is to mine your life for a subject that will pour out instead of trickle.

Different people prefer different brainstorming methods. Below, you'll find explanations of several different methods. Maybe one method will do the trick for you, or maybe you'll find that some combination of methods works best.

Make a List

Many people prefer to begin by making a list. Begin by simply jotting down a list of possible essay topics. After you have a long list, go back and pick out the most promising ideas.

Connect the Words

If you think visually, you might want to try brainstorming by writing a word or phrase in the middle of a blank piece of paper. Spend ten minutes looking at this word or phrase and writing down everything that comes to mind. Stop when your ideas stop flowing. Then circle or draw lines between ideas that are connected. Do this again with a clean sheet of paper with a new word or with a word from your first list. Repeat as necessary.

Here are some sample prompts from the Common Application and from a few specific schools. Notice anything similar? Each prompt is so broad that you could write about virtually anything you want—and that's the point. Admissions committees want to see the real you. The freedom to pick a topic gives you a great opportunity to show off who you are, what you think, and what you believe.

Essay Prompts from the Common Application

- Evaluate a significant experience, achievement, risk you have taken, or ethical dilemma you have faced and its impact on you.

- Discuss some issue of personal, local, national, or international concern and its importance to you.

- Indicate a person who has had a significant influence on you and describe that influence.

- Describe a character in fiction, an historical figure, or creative work (as in art, music, science, etc.) that has had an influence on you and explain that influence.

- A range of academic interests, personal perspectives, and life experiences adds much to the educational mix. Given your personal background, describe an experience that illustrates what you would bring to the diversity in the college community or an encounter that demonstrated the importance of diversity to you.

- Topic of your choice.

Not-So-Common Essay Prompts

- According to astronomer Carl Sagan, "Somewhere, something incredible is waiting to be known." What unknown would you like to see revealed in your lifetime? Why is this of personal importance? (Northwestern University)

- In *The Moviegoer*, a novel by Carolina alumnus Walker Percy, the narrator observes: "The search is what anyone would undertake if he were not stuck in the everydayness of his own life. . . . To become aware of the possibility of the search is to be onto something. Not to be onto something is to be in despair." Are you "onto something" now? If so, what is that something, and why is it important to you? (University of North Carolina)

- On Mars, the latest TV fad among the native lifeforms is *Trading Bodies*. You're picked to play. Whose body would you inhabit and why? (University of Virginia)

- Have you witnessed a person who is close to you doing something that you considered seriously wrong? Describe the circumstances, your thoughts, and how you chose to respond. If you discussed it with the person, was his/her justification valid? In retrospect, what, if anything, would you have done differently and why? (Duke University)

- Do you believe there's a generation gap? Describe the differences between your generation and others. (Denison University)

- What is your academic passion? (Wake Forest University)

WAYS To Get Started

To get the ball rolling on your topic search, write about:

1

The 10 coolest places you've visited

2

Your 10 most memorable high school experiences

3

The 5 most difficult moments in your life

4

The 5 most exciting moments

5

The 3 most awkward moments

6

Your 5 best accomplishments

7

The top 5 words your parents, friends, or teachers would use
to describe you

8

The 5 most important influences on your life

9

Your 5 favorite books

10

Your 10 favorite activities

Draw a Timeline

Here's another visual brainstorming method: write a timeline of your life. Then go back and underline the high and low points. Also, note any other epiphanies or pivotal moments. Don't worry if no single experience changed your life; that's not usually how it works anyway. You can write a thoughtful essay about a change that happened over time, focusing on a particular incident to illustrate your point.

Tell a Story

Pick a word that describes you and write it or type it at the top of a piece of paper. Then write down the title of five stories about yourself that you could tell to illustrate that word. Pick the title you like the most and write that at the top of a new piece of paper. List everything you might include in that story. Imagine the smells, sights, and sounds. Push yourself to come up with all possible details (you can always eliminate some details later). Don't stop until you have exhausted all possibilities.

Freewrite

Some writers call freewriting "the mind dump," because it means dumping everything that comes into your head onto a piece of paper. To freewrite, start with a vague idea, like why your favorite subject is French. For a period of ten or fifteen minutes, write down everything that comes to mind. Don't worry about grammar, style, or making sense. Just keep writing. If you have nothing to say, just write *I have nothing to say* over and over again until something else pops in your head. When the time is up up, take a break and then go back and reread your words. Underline everything that is interesting or promising. Freewrite as much as you like until you have a good crop of ideas.

"I fervently believe that everyone has a story. Not everyone is comfortable telling it, but everyone has one."

Gary Ross
Dean of Admissions,
Colgate University

Brainstorming
Questions

1

What was your most frightening experience?

2

Whom do you love?

3

What books have changed your life?

4

What is your favorite season? Why?

5

Have you ever had a sudden realization about yourself? What was it?

6

What has been the biggest disappointment in your life so far?

7

What kind of art inspires you?

8

What is the kindest thing you've ever done for someone else?

9

If you could change anything about your life, what would it be?

10

In what accomplishment do you take the most pride?

After the Brainstorm

You came up with a bunch of ideas during the brainstorming process, and now you have a few strong potential essay topics. It's time to narrow down your list. Get rid of topics that are too vague (*I'm responsible*) or too narrow (*I've only been late for school three times in four years*). Get rid of topics that are too controversial (*Why Republicans/Democrats are ruining America*) or too risqué (*Why getting high can be exciting*). Save the topics that are interesting and specific (*My summer job researching giant turtles in the South Pacific*). Keep narrowing down until you're left with a topic that will reveal something about you, that you can write about in detail, and that, most important, you'll actually enjoy tackling.

A word of warning: you will probably have many false starts. That's okay! If you've given an idea a fair shot and it's just not working out, try one of the other ideas you came up with during brainstorming. Remember, the admissions committee isn't going to see that overflowing trash can full of drafts and missteps. They're just going to see the finished product.

Pitfalls

Below, you'll find an explanation of how to avoid potential pitfalls when choosing the perfect topic.

The Challenge Question Trap

If you're faced with an essay question about a challenge you've overcome, you might worry to yourself, "I live in a nice house, my parents are nice to me, my grandparents are healthy, and my dog is alive. What do I know about challenges?" Even if your life hasn't been that hard, you have surely faced difficulties of some kind—striving for something and failing, for example, or trying to do the right thing even if it's unpopular. Your challenge may

Worn-Out Topics

1

The Big Game

2

My Trip Abroad

3

Outward Bound

4

Death of a relative

5

Comparing oneself to food

6

Volunteering

7

Poverty

8

Racism

9

Equality

10

World Peace

have been getting along with a sibling, developing character, or balancing studies with activities.

All you can do is rely on your own life experiences for material. Admissions officers will be perfectly happy to read an interesting, strong essay about a less-than-tragic challenge. So you don't need to panic if your brainstorming didn't yield any truly insurmountable challenges—just work with what you have. Colleges understand that you are only seventeen or eighteen years old and that you may not have had the opportunity to travel abroad or leave your hometown. Ultimately, what they care about is good writing. If you write a good essay, what you have will be enough.

The Cliché Trap

We've said it before and we'll say it again: the admissions officers have a lot of reading to do. Entertain them with vivid, clear writing and original ideas, and you'll win their hearts. Bore them with yet another essay about how an Outward Bound trip allowed your inner strength to blossom, and in their minds you'll merge with all the other students who wrote about that topic. What's worse, if another applicant writes a Pulitzer Prize–worthy essay about Outward Bound, yours may pale in comparison.

Admissions officers have read thousands of essays about the exhilaration of scoring the winning touchdown, the lessons learned from volunteering in impoverished areas, and the new perspectives gained from traveling abroad. If you want to write about one of these topics, leave in a little texture: admit that things still aren't perfect. If your story is about flawlessly perfect behavior or sober lessons learned, the admissions office will let out a collective yawn. Being flawed but lovable is more interesting than being a charitable cheerleader with perfect grades.

Avoid Popular Topics

"I love lacrosse, soccer and hockey games as much as anyone, but there's not too much to learn about an applicant when I read four or five essays a day about how scoring a goal changed someone's life."

Gary Ross
Dean of Admissions,
Colgate University

10
Dangerous Topics

1

Sex

2

Suicide attempts

3

Anorexia

4

Depression

5

Drugs

6

Alcohol

7

Vandalism

8

Theft

9

Violence

10

Terrorism

In the battle to avoid cliché, use details. If you play basketball, don't write about how playing on the team has taught you how to be a team player. Any guy on any team in any high school can write about that. Talk about a specific moment you experienced and what effect it had on you. For example, recount the time you went one for ten and shot five air balls. Describe the gasps you heard emanating from the stands each time you missed a shot. Additionally, set the scene with details that give context. Talk about the rubbery smack of the ball on the parquet, and the way your legs feel like they're filled with seltzer water on the night before a big game. When you're picking your topic, make sure you're picking one you can write about in great and vivid detail.

"[From the essay] we can get an idea of how capable the applicant is as a writer, how thoughtful she is as an individual, and how well she responds to assignments that are presented to her."

Gary Ross
Dean of Admissions,
Colgate University

The Temptingly Lofty Topic Trap

Talking about a national or international issue that you feel strongly about can showcase your intelligence and insight and prove that you are thoughtful and knowledgeable. Don't worry about whether the entire admissions committee will agree with everything you write. If you are able to form an argument and support it well, you will win the respect of the admissions officers even if their opinions differ from yours.

Many applicants make the mistake of trying to impress admissions officers by writing about a lofty topic even if they know next to nothing about it. Unless you are truly impassioned about a major issue or personally involved in it in some way, your essay will wind up sounding phony and pious. Essays full of vague platitudes (*In my opinion, there is no nobler cause than fighting to eliminate homelessness*) will not bring you to life for the admissions officers. A better tactic is to be honest and write about something you know well. Don't be afraid to show the admissions officers your true self. That is, after all, the point.

MEMOIRS

Reading someone else's life story is a great way
to get inspired for writing your personal essay.

1

Anna Quindlen, *How Reading Changed My Life*

2

Russell Baker, *Growing up*

3

E. B. White, *The Age of Dust*

4

Joan Didion, *On Going Home*

5

George Orwell, *Shooting an Elephant*

6

Amy Tan, *Mother Tongue*

7

Tobias Wolff, *This Boy's Life*

8

Max Apple, *Roommates*

9

Edward Hoagland, *The Courage of Turtles*

10

Susanna Kaysen, *Girl, Interrupted*

The Vagueness Trap

Don't forget to keep the focus on you. "Whether you are writing about your favorite book, an influential person, or your favorite subject, remember that your essay needs to convey something about you to the college," says Kelly Tanabe, cofounder of SuperCollege.com. If, for example, you write about your grandfather, keep in mind that the way you portray him and the traits you admire in him are a reflection of your own values.

Whatever You Do, Don't

- **Try to pass off a paper you wrote for school as an application essay.** The admissions office will be able to tell that you didn't expend the time or energy necessary to craft a thoughtful response to their question.

- **Use gimmicks.** Sending in a collection of your Calvin and Hobbes–inspired cartoons may show that you are creative, but it doesn't show your writing ability, and it will almost certainly annoy the admissions officers. You'll stand out with sophisticated thoughts and your grammatical and readable writing, not with gimmicks or painfully inappropriate creativity.

- **Be flippant.** "One of the worst essays I ever read was one where the applicant wrote: 'You didn't give me a topic to write on so I have nothing to say,'" remembers Margret Korzus, Associate Dean of Admissions at the University of Denver. Don't act like you're above the process.

3

THE STRUCTURE

"Many students view themselves as victims of the college essay. Don't fall into that role. Think of yourself as the CEO of your college essay."

Margaret Korzus
Associate Dean of Admissions,
University of Denver

When you write a personal essay, you don't have to follow the rigid five-paragraph structure you learned in ninth grade: an introduction, three pieces of evidence, and a conclusion. The college application essay allows you more freedom.

In this chapter we will look at different structural devices and how and when which ones work best. The kind of structural foundation you choose depends in part on your subject matter and on your own personal preference. If you do it well, your structure will help you tell a better story because it will frame your material, creating momentum, and emphasizing your point.

All About You

Some essay prompts ask you to write about an issue or a work of art or literature that is meaningful to you, rather than to recount a personal story. Nonetheless, you should always relate the topic back to yourself. The most effective way to do so is to write a first-person essay and use the pronoun *I* throughout to call attention to your views and experiences. If your essay prompt is to explore the pros and cons of gay marriage, incorporate your life story into the essay and clearly state how the issue relates to you. The first person forces you to discuss why this topic is significant to you, why you believe what you believe, and what, if any, conflicting feelings you have about it.

For example, you can start with a flashback that describes the first time you realized your best friend was gay and then go on to discuss the different sides of the national debate. You could also describe how you used to feel about the issue and how you changed your mind following an event involving your best friend.

Framing Your Essay

Let's say you want to write about how you used to think your little sister was a brat and now you don't. Maybe you had this realization about her one night when you were babysitting and heard a noise that terrified you, and she said something wise and comforting that made you see her in a new light. You could structure your essay in the following ways:

Flashback: You start with a flashback, describing the fear and panic you felt, where you were when you heard the noise, and what thoughts went through your mind. You describe what your sister said and did and how that made you feel. Then you talk about how much this surprised you because, until that moment, you had always thought she was just a big pain and you never gave her a chance.

Cause/Effect: You begin by talking about how your sister used to follow you around and tattle on you all the time. You tell an anecdote about how much she drove you crazy. Then you take the reader through this one event that made you realize how much she has to offer.

These structures overlap a bit. For example, the cause/effect structure is also a narrative, taking the reader through the particular moment in time when your attitude changed. For both options, you might conclude in a similar way, by saying that you look forward to continuing to get to know her as a person as you both grow up. You might even broaden your scope and talk more generally about how it's important to give people a chance or how much you can learn from others if you keep your mind open.

> "All good essayists make use at times of storytelling devices: descriptions of character and place, incident, dialogue, conflict. Even a 'pure' meditation, the track of one's thoughts, has to be shaped, given a kind of plot or urgency, if it is to communicate."
>
> **Phillip Lopate**
> *The Art of the Personal Essay*

10
Narrative Tips

1

Use vivid descriptions.

2

Start and end with action, if appropriate.

3

Keep the story moving forward.

4

Be clear about the chronology of events.

5

Don't give too many details.

6

Include dialogue where appropriate.

7

Use active verbs.

8

Explain why you are telling this story.

9

Be specific.

10

Don't repeat yourself.

Telling a Good Story

Ultimately, your personal essay is a story about you. Think of friends or family members who always tell entertaining anecdotes. Why do you like to hear them recount stories? It's probably not because they list events or recite characteristics of the people they are describing. They pull you immediately into the action and include great dialogue and details, which allow their stories to unfold. Good stories have energy and are insightful without hitting you over the head with their point.

Before you choose your structure, think about how you want the reader to experience your essay and view your material. If you want to provide a glimpse into your life, a narrative structure is probably best. If you want to dazzle your reader with your ability to look at both sides of an issue, go with a pro/con structure. If you want to persuade the reader about a point of view you hold (but remember that admissions officers don't like to be preached to), go with a traditional five-paragraph essay structure.

Now, let's explore your options, along with their strengths and weaknesses. No matter which option you choose, write the entire essay prompt at the top of your draft and refer back to it as you write to make sure you are addressing it.

"Typically students are taught to write in the five-paragraph form. Anyone who goes outside of that automatically draws me in. I want to know, 'Can you draw outside the lines and make it look good?' Alternatively, if you stick to the usual form, I want to know, 'Can you still make it interesting?'"

Meghan Cadwallader Assistant Director of Admissions, Susquehanna University

The Narrative Essay

While admissions officers say there isn't one structure that always works best, when pressed, most agree that the narrative approach is often the most effective and compelling foundation for an essay. Anyone can write a narrative because everyone has a story to tell.

"We want someone who can tell a story that's going to keep our attention, because we just read 800 other essays," says Tim Cheney, Associate Dean of Admissions at

10

First Encounters

When choosing anecdotes to include in your narrative essay, it often helps to start with a first encounter. Here are some ideas:

1
First music lesson

2
First visit to a family member

3
First day of school

4
First time seeing a new sibling

5
First trip abroad

6
First driving lesson

7
First religious ceremony

8
First job

9
First big win

10
First big loss

Connecticut College. "People often try different stylistic approaches," he says, but a lot of them flop. "A straight-up solid narrative is probably going to get you the most value."

A narrative approach is useful when you focus on a single event. You can also trace the origin and development of a particular passion by describing several brief scenes relating to it. But don't try to cover a long period of time. You know those people who tell stories with too many details that take too long to tell? Don't be one of them.

Here is the introduction to an essay that uses the narrative approach:

My dad and I are driving down the winding South Carolina roads. We're on the six-hour drive from Atlanta to Edisto, and it's midnight now. We're over halfway there. A heavy layer of fog lingers in the air around our car, clearly defining our headlight beams as they hit the moist particles. The curving road is desolate and unlighted, but occasionally, as we round its bend, a truck approaches from the opposite direction. We squint at its blinding headlights as my dad flicks off our brights. This occasional trucker is the only other human life form we see.

The trees that line the road, however, seem nearly human; their armlike branches bend toward our car as if they are trying to pluck us from the road. The passenger side window is cold and a curtain of condensation hinders my view. I pull the sleeve of my sweatshirt over my hand and wipe a frosty layer off the glass so that I can see the passing trees. Our windshield wipers provide the only sound: an eerie rhythmic pumping. Eyes wide, I turn to my dad, a smile spreading across my face. "This is the perfect setting for a scary movie," I say, and I could not be happier.

Survey of Events vs. Focusing on a Single Event

One way to approach a narrative is to tell various relevant anecdotes that prove your point. Let's say you are writing about your role model, your great-aunt Matilda. You could start with your first memory of Aunt Matilda and then go on to describe several moments when she taught you important lessons, ending with a more recent event involving Aunt Matilda.

However, you need to be careful as the survey approach can get a little boring. It is usually more powerful to hone in on a single, specific event. The very act of applying more intensive focus will imbue it with more meaning.

Flashback

When you use a flashback to start your narrative essay, you can use the body of the essay to reflect on how that past experience shaped who you are today.

If you choose this approach, consider ending with a different part of the original scene than what you used as your introductory paragraph. For example, let's say you are writing about a road trip you took with your father. You start with the two of you in a gas station, lost and asking for directions. The rest of the essay is then about what you learned about yourself on that trip with your father. Consider ending the essay with the two of you in that same gas station but at another moment in time. Maybe after you got the directions, you climbed into the driver's seat, instead of the passenger's seat, and claimed your role as an adult.

"It's important that someone who has never experienced whatever you are talking about can understand what's going on. If you are flashing back or forward, make sure it's clear. Have someone else read it to see if they understand the order of events," advises Meghan Cadwallader, Assistant Director of Admissions at Susquehanna University.

The Compare/Contrast Essay

This structure showcases your ability to analyze a topic. You might use it to discuss an issue of importance to you, exploring two different solutions to a problem and explaining the pros and cons of each.

You can also use this method to compare and contrast two people and their different influences on you. For example, maybe your maternal grandfather was a rabbi and your paternal grandfather was a fireman. While they were wildly different in demeanor, background, religious belief, and physical appearance, they both taught you the importance of helping others.

Shades of Gray

An essay that examines the pros and cons of an issue can show that you are thoughtful, open-minded, and able to see more than one side of an issue. But you should only use this structure if you are actually open-minded enough about the topic to see the shades of gray. You'd want to show why the issue matters to you and then look at both sides before offering your final thoughts. If you are still conflicted about the topic, there's nothing wrong with saying so.

For example, if you are writing about the pros and cons of reinstating the military draft, you could first write about how mandatory service in the army would instill a sense of civic pride in people. Then you could counter this by saying that a draft would force people to enlist even if they are philosophically opposed to the military. The bulk of your argument should be nuanced, explaining how a pro could be con, and vice versa. You might note that while military service helps people from poorer communities pay for college, it also means people with less money are more likely to die in combat.

The Traditional Essay

As we've discussed, the traditional academic essay is five paragraphs long. It starts with a thesis statement and introduction, continues with three pieces of evidence that support the argument, and concludes with a paragraph explaining what the essay has illustrated.

This structure works well when you're trying to prove a point: it is strong and simple, and it allows you to illustrate several pieces of supporting

10
COMPARE/CONTRAST
Tips

1

Stay on topic.

2

Explain why the topic is important to you.

3

Explain how the topic has affected you personally.

4

Be insightful.

5

Explore every side thoroughly.

6

Don't jump to judgments.

7

Point out where things overlap.

8

Focus on the gray areas.

9

Offer perspectives that aren't obvious to the reader.

10

Keep it simple.

evidence. You can use the traditional structure to answer most of the Common Application questions. For example, let's say you're answering this prompt:

Evaluate a significant experience, achievement, risk you have taken, or ethical dilemma you have faced and its impact on you.

Your thesis could be:

My parents' divorce taught me to see them for the first time as people separate from me, with their own sets of emotions, needs, and desires.

The next three paragraphs would offer examples of how you see them as people, not just parents, and you'd conclude with a restatement of your thesis in the fifth paragraph.

While it is useful for making a persuasive argument, the traditional academic structure can be too formulaic for a college essay. You might produce a successful essay based on this structure, but a narrative structure or a compare/contrast essay will infuse the story with more energy.

The Inventive Essay Structure

Oftentimes an essay prompt asks you to write something creative, like an obituary for yourself or a page from your autobiography. While the admissions officers who read these essays clearly want to see your creativity, there should still be a main point to what you're writing. Ask yourself whether your creative essay reveals something about you. If it doesn't, then you're not giving the admissions officers a glimpse into who you are and why you would be a valuable member of their school's academic community.

The most successful inventive essays use a form that showcases the content. A person interested in creative writing might choose to highlight that interest by submitting her essay as a long poem. Some schools, particularly those specializing in the visual arts, might ask you to submit only a brief statement of intent (like an essay) and focus instead on a portfolio of your work. Their applications will clearly state if this is the case. For an example of an inventive essay that really worked, see the screenplay structure of a real essay in Chapter 10.

4
THE ROUGH DRAFT

"Almost all good writing begins with terrible first efforts. You need to start somewhere. Start by getting something—anything—down on paper."

Anne Lamott
Bird by Bird

WAYS
To Fight
Procrastination

1

Work in a quiet space, without distractions.

2

Write first thing in the morning or right before you go to bed.

3

Carry a writing notebook with you, and write when you feel inspired.

4

Turn off your phone's ringer.

5

Turn off your internet access.

6

Tell your parents when you are writing so they don't disturb you.

7

Don't write when you're hungry.

8

Don't stay up late to write.

9

Don't write when you have a lot of schoolwork to complete.

10

Start writing with some idea of what you want to say.

You've already done a lot of the hard work. You've clarified your topic and collected as many ideas as you can, and you have specific scenes you want to describe and details to include. Now it's time to write the rough draft.

The first thing you should do is give yourself an early deadline. Make sure to leave enough time to write several drafts; get feedback from a teacher, relative, or friend; make revisions based on those comments; take a few days off; and proofread several times.

Ideally, you will have started working on your essay over the summer, and your rough draft will be done before you begin senior year. If your summer is packed with activity, you should start work on your essay as soon as the school year starts and have a complete rough draft by the end of September.

Procrastination

When you settle in at your desk and turn on your computer, don't be surprised if you suddenly find yourself desperate for a glass of water or a bowl of ice cream. Maybe you'll start to feel a little chilly and need to get up and put on a sweater. You may feel compelled to write your grandmother that thank-you note, clean your closet, walk the dog, or even do your calculus homework. This desire to do anything other than to write is perfectly normal. Nothing is more daunting than a blank computer screen.

All writers feel anxious when they have to start writing. The best cure? *Begin writing.*

Perfectionism

Your rough draft doesn't have to be perfect. It doesn't even have to be good. Nobody ever has to see it. When you are writing your rough draft, give yourself permission to write poorly. This is your opportunity to explore your thoughts and ideas without worrying about how they sound. This is not the time to focus on word choice or organization. The idea is just to get your thoughts out of your head and onto paper or computer screen so you have something to work with.

If you took notes while you were brainstorming and developing your topic, try turning the notes about each subtopic into a paragraph or several paragraphs. Imagine that you are telling a friend, sibling, parent, or favorite teacher about the topic. Without worrying about perfect structure or language, write down the words as if you were speaking.

Write quickly; don't censor your thoughts. Use whatever words come to you. Don't deliberate over every word or sentence. Just type whatever pops into your head. Remember, this is a rough draft. You'll be going back later to figure out if there's a better word or a better way of phasing your ideas.

Grammar and Spelling

Don't worry about grammar and spelling for now. You can go back and fix that later too. Even if those squiggly red lines appear underneath a word telling you that you've misspelled it, or if you just wrote something awkward, irrelevant, or inappropriate, don't delete it or go back and fix it. Just keep forging ahead. The more words you can get down, the better. It's always easier to cut than to add.

The Skeleton

You can only organize your essay if you have something to work with. Think of it this way: you couldn't clean or reorder your room unless you had a whole mess of stuff all over the place. For now, you'll be working on getting all your thoughts out, without getting mired in the mechanics of writing or the details of your story.

At this point, you are creating what is known as "the skeleton." You don't even need to be concerned about the facts. If you are not sure about a detail, you can put in a question mark, make a note to yourself, or leave a blank. Nothing is etched in stone.

Sample Skeleton

Topic: Personal Statement on Racial Identity

The hardest part about taking the SAT was filling out the section on race. All the other students knew what to write, but I was confused and upset.

Everyone assumes I'm white because of my light skin, and they are always surprised when I tell them I'm actually black. Do I wish my skin were darker or I looked more obviously black? No, for me being black is about my culture and my family. My grandfather worked for ???? newspaper in Chicago, the oldest black newspaper in America.

At the same time I identify with the Irish side of my family too. My father's family came from Ireland to Ellis Island in ??? (can't remember the year: ask DAD)

Other ideas:

Write about the incident during sexual awareness day at school when the lecturer assumed I was a blond, white girl.

Census forms and racial questionnaires oversimplify people's identity.

Getting Started

To get things started, give yourself a brief amount of time to write freely and as quickly as you can. Tell yourself that you have to stay put in your chair and write for fifteen minutes, without checking your email, downloading another song off the internet, or asking your mom what's for dinner.

After fifteen minutes, you can take a five-minute break to reward yourself and clear your mind. Soon you will find that you can write for longer intervals, maybe twenty minutes, then a half hour or even an hour. It's good writing practice to set up an allotted period of time and be disciplined enough to stick to it.

Writing can be cathartic, especially when you are writing about a topic close to your heart. Think of it as getting your emotional energy out. Instead of stressing, try to focus on the task at hand. As Duke Ellington said, "I merely took the energy it takes to pout and wrote some blues."

Taking Breaks

You're probably not going to write your entire rough draft in a single session. That is perfectly fine. Breaks are an important part of the creative process. Breaks will keep you awake, alert, and fresh. You can take breaks to reward yourself for finishing a section or if you're feeling a little stuck.

It seems natural to take a break at the end of a paragraph. But some people like to stop in the middle of a paragraph or a section, so they don't have to start a completely new task when they go back to it. This is a matter of personal preference.

If possible, try to be smart about when you take your breaks. Before abandoning your computer, first try to jot down any other ideas that may have been floating around in your head that you didn't get to yet. This way when you sit down tomorrow or next week, the words will jog your memory.

Don't examine every
word before going
to the next one, edit
or delete what you
just wrote, on pause
to worry about
grammar, spelling,
or organization.
Otherwise you'll
never be able to
move forward and
get all your ideas
down—which is the
point of the rough
draft.

The Draft

There's no easy way to define a *rough* draft. For some people, it will include complete sentences with fully formed
thoughts. For others, a rough draft will be phrases pieced
together. The most important thing is that you write in a
way that allows you to go back later and understand what
you were trying to get across.

Here are two examples of a rough draft. You'll have a
chance to see the final, polished versions in Chapter 10:

1. **Essay prompt: Describe a personal challenge you
   overcame.**

   *My first day working at Gino's restaurant was terrifying. I was so
   excited to get a job working at a restaurant, but I had no idea what I
   was getting myself into. The manager, Morizio (spelling?) took me to
   the basement, and on the way down a waitress yelled at me. I was a
   lowly busboy.*

   *Down there, there were two men folding napkins. This was to be
   my job too. I thought I knew what I was doing so I didn't bother asking for help. Pretty soon it was obvious to everyone that I didn't know
   what I was doing.*

   *[add some dialogue here, maybe some of the Italian
   I learned in the restaurant?]*

   *A waiter asked me to get a cappuccino for a customer. Again, I was
   afraid to ask so I just made it myself. It was a disaster. When they
   figured out I was clueless, they got mad that I didn't just say I was
   clueless. There was no winning with these people. What I quickly realized was that my fear of seeming clueless actually made me unable to
   perform my job.*

Everything changed back at school in physics class. We were learning about fiber optics. The teacher said something like "I'm sure you all get this topic, so we'll move on." My experience in the restaurant taught me to speak up and say, "No, I don't get. Can you please explain?" The teacher happily answered my question and I felt a huge sense of relief.

This wasn't a huge, life-changing moment necessarily, but it helped me overcome a crippling fear.

2. **Essay prompt:** **If you could have lunch with any person, living, dead, or fictional, who would it be and what would you discuss?**

The person I'm most intrigued by is Che Guevara, the revolutionary leader who ended his medical career to fight for poor people in Cuba.

I imagine Che wanting to meet at a small restaurant in one of the poorer neighborhoods of Chicago. Maybe that small Mexican place by the El downtown. . . . (that place where I watched the World Cup last year).

We would discuss politics and how/if things have improved in Latin America. This was his stated goal, so it'd be interesting to find out if he thinks the "revolution" was a success. If he says yes, I'll challenge him and say poverty still exists and that there is political repression in Cuba. I agree a lot with his politics, but I think the issue is more global than just Latin America.

I'm most curious about why the revolution never moved beyond Cuba. Che will have some insights on this, based on all the foreign intervention in Latin America, especially by the U.S.

Maybe discuss September 11, but not in much detail? Tie it to violence, which I don't think is a means to a justifiable end. Does he think so? There was a lot of violence around the revolution in Cuba.

In the end, I realize he is just another person, and his early death and celebrity are what make him seem so untouchable.

Wait on the Intro

Many students make the mistake of trying to write the introduction first. Sounds logical, right? But if you think about it, it would be impossible to introduce something if you haven't clearly defined what it is you're

10

THINGS

You Don't Gotta
Worry About . . . Yet!

introducing. In other words, once you get all your ideas down and start to look at what you've written, you will then have a much better sense of where your essay is really going. Even though you may have predetermined your topic and what you want to focus on, you will only really see your ideas start to shape up once you've started to write. You can write a much better intro once you've fleshed out your ideas. You will never start the essay if you belabor how to begin.

When you get someone else to read your rough draft, or when you go back to revise it yourself, one of you will probably find the perfect first sentence buried somewhere in the middle or even toward the end of your draft. Most writers find that when they go back to revise, they discover the hook that will draw in the reader. Similarly, many writers wait until later to find a good conclusion somewhere in their first draft. We will go into more detail about both the introduction and the conclusion in Chapter 5.

Save Your Drafts

When you start working on a new draft, save the file from the last version you worked on with a new name, according to the date or the draft (Essay_draft1, Essay_draft2, etc.). That way you can go back to an old draft and find any sections that you may have deleted and still need.

Digging Deeper

While you are writing, try to do more than just state the facts. This is the time to try and take your ideas further. If you think you don't have anything else to say, look at what you've jotted down and ask yourself: "So what?" Why is what you said important? What did it teach you? What does it mean? What are the broader implications?

So What?

Suppose you are writing a description of someone you admire. You are able to describe that person in detail: she has big brown eyes and a beautiful smile; she wears stylish clothes and walks with a confident gait. How do you dig deeper? What exactly do you admire about her beyond her physical attributes or her clothes? Does she have a

10

SO WHAT
Questions

1

Why is your topic important to you?

2

Why did you choose your details?

3

Why should you keep these details in your essay?

4

How do your anecdotes enrich your essay?

5

What do your descriptions say about you?

6

How are the people you discuss meaningful to you?

7

Why are you focusing on a particular moment in time?

8

How did you form your opinions?

9

Will your readers understand the connections you make?

10

What more can you say to dig deeper?

way of speaking or expressing herself in an unusual way? Why do you think she is stylish? Does she dress in an unusual way that you feel is artistic? By going beyond the facts, you will suddenly find more to say that will then be interesting to the reader.

You don't have to have well-formed opinions when you first write down your thoughts. When you work on your next draft, you'll go back and figure out how your ideas connect and make sure there is a unifying principle.

If you are writing about your favorite book, don't just give a plot summary. Think about why the book is important to you and how it has affected the way you look at your life, the world, the environment, your community, or your family. Don't just say you were editor-in-chief of the school newspaper; talk about what kind of editor you were and what factors in your life shaped your approach as an editor.

5

VOICE

"I go to the essay first. I want to know who the person is prior to looking at grades and test scores."

Margret Korzus
Associate Dean of Admissions,
University of Denver

"I always read the essay last because I wanted to come away with the student's voice in my head."

Eric Furda
Former Director of Undergraduate Admissions,
Columbia University

Your writing voice is the personality that comes across when someone reads your essay. Your word choice, tone, and attitude all impact the reader's perception of you. In this chapter, we'll talk about how to get enough distance from your own words to look at the effect they may have on the reader, and how to alter your voice when necessary, while staying true to yourself.

Your Audience

As you know by now, the admissions officers are your audience—your "customers," so to speak—and they want to know that you can write. But they also really want to know what sort of person you are. Will you be a considerate roommate? Will you add an interesting perspective to the classroom? Will you be a thoughtful and productive member of the school's community?

"We are looking for potential contributors to campus life. As we try to shape the class, it's important to think about the personality of our campus and who we'd like to see here," says Brad Ward, Associate Director of Admissions at Bucknell University.

Being Yourself

You need to be comfortable with the language and tone you use. "Getting too much coaching can work against a student because then she's not being true to her own voice. We're looking for the student's voice, and a 30-year-old and a 40-year-old sound different from a 17-year-old," says Eric Furda, Former Director of Undergraduate Admissions at Columbia University.

Admissions officers expect the essay to confirm what they have already learned about you from reading the rest of your application. They view each part of the application as a piece of evidence and, just like in a courtroom, all the evidence must make sense and fit together logically.

"When students try to be someone they're not, thinking they are going to impress us, it backfires," says Francis Gummere, Director of Alumni Admissions Programs at Lake Forest College. "When someone's transcript reflects all Cs in English, and then all of the sudden you get a brilliant piece of writing, guess what? The flags are zipping up and down the flagpole, and they are red."

Authenticity

Your essay should reflect who you really are, not who you think the admissions officers want you to be," says Eric Furda. "It's important to be authentic. If you have a certain style, you should probably stick with it. Some people say, 'I'll make a splash by doing something different or shocking.' That's fine if that's who you are, but if it's not, you're stretching, and not in an appropriate manner. The essay is about showing who you are, what you're about, what motivates you, what you value, and your ability to communicate these things in writing. It's about the student, the person, the individual who's going to be someone's classmate, roommate, and teammate. The essay is another dimension to who the individual is. Some essays may be a little more whimsical, and that's fine, if that's who you are." Bottom line: know thy self, and put that self into your essay.

Consistency

We all use different speaking styles depending on to whom we are speaking. If you are talking to your best friend, the words and tone you choose are not the same as those you'd use when speaking to your high school principal, your favorite aunt, or your love interest. Without thinking about it, we all move naturally between styles when we speak.

In your rough draft, your goal was simply to get the words and thoughts out on the paper, so you probably used the voice that is most comfortable for you. At times, you might have even shifted back and forth between styles.

Go through your essay to determine whether the voice you use in each section is the most effective way to convey your point. Do you sound like yourself? Does your voice shift so drastically that it sounds like two different people wrote the essay? That will set off alarms and could possibly hurt your chances of getting in. Changes in tone and inconsistent style could suggest that people were helping you with parts of your essay.

10

Characteristics of Good Essays

1
Confident

2
Relaxed

3
Reflective

4
Genuine

5
Friendly

6
Self-aware

7
Optimistic

8
Natural

9
Direct

10
Engaging

Tone

Your tone isn't set in stone. One way to think about tone is to see it as the mood behind your essay. We all have many moods, but we don't necessarily reveal all our moods to just anyone. If, for example, you happened to lose your cell phone right before you were meeting your boyfriend's mother for the first time, you'd probably manage to speak to her in a pleasant and friendly voice even if you were upset about the phone. In the same way that we have to control our moods, we need to control our tone in our writing.

It's not about being phony. It's about presenting your best self to the admissions officers. Your essay should sound like your most inspired conversation. "What frustrates me is when kids don't take advantage of the opportunity to present themselves well," says Francis Gummere.

10 Pitfalls

How can you make sure the voice you are using is your own? First, read your essay out loud. Does it sound like you, or does it sound like a machine trying to get into college? Don't try to impress the reader with big words or big concepts. Your writing voice should sound a lot like your speaking voice, only more polished.

There are a lot of mistakes when it comes to voice. In the rest of this chapter, we will explore the most common ones and show you how to avoid them.

"The personal essay has historically sought to puncture the stiffness of formal discourse with language that is casual, everyday, demotic, direct."

Phillip Lopate
The Art of the
Personal Essay

Mistake #1: Fancy Words

"Many promising essays are sabotaged by wordiness," says Margret Korzus, Associate Dean of Admissions at the University of Denver. "In an attempt to sound sophisticated and authoritative, college applicants often make the mistake of using flowery, formal words they'd never use when speaking. The result is an essay that reads as phony and sounds like the applicant is trying too hard."

While the occasional *pulchritude* instead of *beauty* can be effective, too many can make you sound stiff and stuffy. "You don't want to come off as if you have a thesaurus in your hand and you are using words that not only a 17-year-old wouldn't use but that most people wouldn't use. That's a mistake," says Eric Furda. "But it comes back to who you really are. There are many bright students with an incredible range of vocabulary, and if that's who you are, then you should use it because we'll pick it up in other parts of the application. But if you have a B– in English and a 580 Verbal on your SAT, we'll wonder."

> **Don't say:** *As my grandmother's physical condition vitiated, I grew increasingly pusillanimous. When she ultimately evanesced, I was, needless to say, infelicitous, yet I remained obdurate that I would withhold from ululating.*

> **Say:** *As my grandmother's illness became more serious, I worried how I would cope with her death. When she finally died, I vowed not to cry in spite of my deep grief.*

Mistake #2: Recycling Brochure Copy

No doubt you have been inundated with brochures describing how "diverse" and "unique" each campus is and how each has a "one-of-a-kind faculty." Don't spit elegant clichés back at the college. If you are going to talk about the college, insert your own experiences or impressions. Don't tell the admissions officers something they already know about their school. It will come across as a shameless attempt at flattery.

> **Don't say:** *I want to go to Dartmouth because it is one of the oldest and most respected universities in the United States with a long history of dedication to the highest educational ideals.*

> **Say:** *On my visit to Dartmouth, I was a guest at a class on the United States Constitution. I was on the edge of my seat for the entire ninety minutes. I had never imagined that a class could be so exciting and students so engaged. Later on during my visit my host student took me to a party, where the room buzzed with similar intelligence and energy. I knew before the weekend was over that I wanted to be a part of the Dartmouth experience.*

Mistake #3: Sense of Entitlement

Try to step back, get some distance, and make sure your essay doesn't come across as if you deserve to get in just because you are who you are—even if you have a perfect GPA, SAT scores in the 99th percentile, a dad who just donated a new gym to the university, and several generations of alumni in your family. The admissions officers are seeking to shape the personality of the class, and they are likely to decide that an arrogant and entitled student might not make the best classmate, roommate, or teammate.

There is a separate space on the application to bring up that you are a legacy; there's no need to harp on it in the essay. If you must mention it, try to show some humility.

Don't say: *Ever since my granddaddy, sitting in his Harvard rocking chair with me on his knee, spoke of his days at Harvard, I knew without a doubt that I too would someday be a part of the Crimson tradition.*

Say: *You might not find it surprising that a kid who grew up in a house with a Harvard rocking chair in the study, banners from the Class of '57 and '35 hanging in the attic playroom, and Crimson needlepoint pillows on the couch in the living room would apply early decision to Harvard. But the truth is that until last year, I was adamantly opposed to going to Harvard. I didn't want to follow in my father's and grandfather's footsteps. I wanted to be different, to forge my own path. Over the past year, however, in spite of myself, I've developed an appreciation of Harvard separate from my family tradition.*

Mistake #4: Boastfulness

There's a fine line between confidence and boastfulness. Instead of talking broadly about how much you've grown, which can come off as self-righteous, describe a specific event that taught you something.

Imagine you are meeting someone for the first time. Would you dive right into a monologue about how wonderful you are? Probably not. A person who is able to reflect on a specific experience with humility, using words that come naturally, is much more likeable. Admissions officers say that some students try to impress them with a sales pitch and formal prose, and they end up sounding pretentious, arrogant, and grating.

"I am moved by essays that have that element of self-awareness, a sense that there is going to be a step after this, an understanding that there is a larger process [beyond the college application process] and there are things they can learn in college," says Richard DiFeliciantonio, Vice President for Enrollment at Ursinus College.

Don't say: *I've grown tremendously in my four years of high school, academically, musically, athletically, and socially.*

Say: *When my freshman English teacher gave me a C- on my first composition, I thought my world had come to an end. I was terrified to tell my parents, and I worried that I would have to abandon my dreams of college and law school. I was a bit melodramatic, I'll admit, but up until that moment in my academic career, I had only gotten As. That grade traumatized me, but it also taught me several important lessons.*

Mistake #5: Simplistic Writing

Another mistake is oversimplifying your argument. As we've said before, you need to dig deeper so your true personality can really shine through. Aim a little more at paradox instead of trying to have everything fit neatly into clear categories. For example, instead of writing *I turned a bad situation into a good thing and everything is great now*, write, *I turned a bad situation into a better thing, but I still really don't like x, y, or z about it.*

Here's an opportunity for you to finally employ some creativity and apply some of the more interesting writing techniques you've learned in high school. Unlike an English or research paper, everything does NOT need to be black-and-white or authoritative.

Don't say: *I have fully recovered from any sorrow about my parents' divorce. It taught me that everything happens for a reason.*

Say: *Divorce brings pain to the entire family. I'll always wish that it hadn't happened, but I am thankful that my parents have both been able to continue their lives and form new relationships and that I have learned to share in their new happiness.*

Mistake #6: Bleached Personality

Don't bleach your personality. If you have trouble finding your voice or being yourself, find a way to work in some habit you may have. Perhaps you bite your nails, for example. It's OK to reveal something imperfect about yourself. It helps the reader say, "This is a human being."

> **Don't say:** *I have always loved school, new experiences, meeting people, and challenging myself, so I can't wait to go to college.*

> **Say:** *While I have some talents, singing on key is not one of them. So when my Italian host family begged me to stand up on stage in front of seventy-five friends and family members and sing the American national anthem, I scanned the room for possible escape routes.*

Mistake #7: Inappropriate Humor

Being funny always makes for a good read. But all admissions officers warn against trying to be funny when you're not.

Certain kinds of humor work better than others. Humor that debases someone is not going to be appreciated. Instead, strive for humor that exposes something comical or ironic about yourself or the world in general. "Think about who you would want to have as a roommate. A person who demeans others will demean you. Be careful that your attempts at humor do not come off as immature or prejudiced," says Margret Korzus.

"Humor, irony, and satire are powerful tools, but they can also backfire. Be very careful with humorous essays unless you have that kind of ability. Err on the side of clear and concise rather than trying to be outrageous or funny. Once we had a candidate who wrote, 'And if I don't get admitted to University of Denver I have to commit suicide.'"

Margret Korzus
Associate Dean
of Admissions,
University of Denver

Don't say: *The only way I can get a date is if I pay the girl. Every now and then a girl is desperate enough to buy a new pair of Seven jeans that she will go out with me. I respect a girl who goes out with a guy for cash. After all, she has weighed her priorities and decided that making out with me, as unpalatable as she might find it to be, is something she can put up with if it means she can wear cute jeans the next night on a date with a guy she really likes.*

Say: *My mother can't understand why all the girls aren't crazy about me. She assures me that once I get to college my charms (skinny arms, pimples, thick glasses, mediocre athletic skills, a passion for classical music) will be appreciated by the opposite sex. So far, I have seen only evidence to the contrary.*

Mistake #8: Flippancy

"Applicants often employ sarcasm in an attempt to be clever. I remember an essay that, in my opinion, backfired. It was along the lines of 'Why I Think Writing Application Essays Is Stupid,'" says Colorado College's Associate Director of Admissions, Ellen Goulding.

When writing something flippant, you might think you're showing how unique you are, but, in fact, enough people take this approach that it is far from original or refreshing. The bottom line is: if you don't answer the question, or if you think you are above the process, you're taking a risk.

"There are times when you open a file and it screams at you, 'I have applied because my momma made me apply.' It screams, 'I'm not interested in your school and I won't enroll if you admit me, please don't admit me.' And we oblige them," says Francis Gummere.

Don't say: *I don't have anything to say that you haven't already read, so I'm not going to waste my time or yours. Just look at my transcript and I think you'll see all the information you need.*

Say: *Anything else!*

Mistake #9: Overstatement

Your voice needs to have energy. A flat, depressed, lifeless voice is not going to win anyone over. At the same time, going overboard with your enthusiasm can be a turnoff too. Admissions officers will certainly not be fooled by enthusiasm if deep down inside you really don't care and they'll recognize your "enthusiasm" as phoniness. But if you are truly passionate about your topic (and you should be), you don't want to come off as being over the top. "People get carried away and we wonder, 'Is this genuine or sincere?' Being too overwrought about something interferes with what you're trying to say ultimately," says Meghan Cadwallader.

> **Don't say:** *I read everything I can get my hands on! If I'm not at school or sleeping, I am reading. I learned to read when I was two years old and I read The Brothers Karamazov over one weekend. Reading has taught me so much, and I would never be who I am if I didn't read as much as I do.*

> **Say:** *I am a voracious reader. My relationship with books has always been perhaps a little more intense than that of my peers. I cherish the way a book feels in my hands, I love the smell when I bury my nose in the spine. At different times in my life different books have inspired me, kept me company, and helped me to cope.*

Mistake #10: Close-Mindedness

Tread with care when you talk about other people in your essay, especially when writing about people from other countries or socioeconomic classes. "Some of the things you say may come off as judgmental or biased, or don't demonstrate a terribly open mind. Avoid making sweeping generalizations, which are often perceived as condescending and close-minded," says Meghan Cadwallader.

Ask the person reviewing your essay to read closely and keep an eye out for places where your voice might sound xenophobic or patronizing—especially if your essay is about your travels in a foreign country or volunteering in the inner city.

> **Don't say:** *In Europe, they don't care as much about cleanliness as we do in America.*

> **Say:** *While I was living with a host family in the French countryside, I was shocked to discover that people only showered twice a week. But I quickly learned that the reason for this practice had nothing to do with cleanliness. Families in this old village have a limited supply of hot water, so they've learned to adapt and conserve.*

G

ORGANIZATION

"The word *essay* comes from the French word *essayer*, which means 'to try.' The ultimate goal of your college essay is to teach or persuade the admission officers by introducing your topic, supporting it in the body of your essay, and bringing it to a conclusion."

Brad Ward
Associate Director of Admissions,
Bucknell University

So, you've finished your rough draft. Congratulations! Pat yourself on the back for getting through a difficult process.

Don't worry if you read your rough draft and it's a bit of a mess: disorganized thoughts, no introduction or conclusion, clunky transitions. That's fine. There's a reason why it's called a *rough draft*. It's important not to get discouraged at this point. Although you still have some work ahead of you, you're on the right track. The rough draft was all about getting your ideas down. Now that you have something to work with, you can go back and create a cohesive, clear, concise, and compelling essay.

When reading this chapter, keep in mind that you're allowed to be creative when writing your essay. The organization we present here should guide your writing, but you can certainly deviate from some of these elements if they don't work with the structure you've chosen. For example, if you're writing a narrative essay that builds toward a conclusion, your main point won't necessarily be explicit in your introductory paragraph. Nonetheless, everything you write should ultimately connect to a unifying theme.

The Main Point

No matter what structure you use for your essay, it should have a main point. In a traditional essay, this element is called the *thesis statement* or, simply, the thesis. If your essay prompt asks you to answer a specific question, your thesis shouldn't just answer the question; it should go deeper and resonate. Some students make the mistake of restating the question. While that may be OK if you are in English class, the application essay is supposed to be an expression of who you are. For example, suppose you are given the following prompt on your application essay:

"Describe the biggest challenge you have faced or expect to face."
Your thesis shouldn't simply state:

The biggest challenge I ever faced was learning how to salsa dance. For your rough draft, that would have been a fine working thesis to get your ideas flowing. But now you need to take your writing to the next level. Think more about the So What? questions we discussed in Chapter 4. See how this thesis statement differs from the previous version:

Learning how to salsa dance may have been the biggest challenge I've ever faced, but it also taught me the importance of patience, humility, and learning how to take the lead.

Is It Relevant?

Your first order of business when you start actually writing your essay is to make sure that the point of your essay is clear. Irrelevant material, no matter how well written or fascinating, will only muddy your argument. One way to determine if you've stayed on track is to write your main point at the top of your first draft and read it through with that point in mind, making sure that everything in the essay relates back to and strengthens your argument.

Paragraphs:
The Building Blocks

The purpose of arranging writing into paragraphs is to organize your information in a way that is understandable to the reader. Unlike your rough drafts, now the information needs to start to make sense to someone other than you. You'll need to scan all your details and start to "build blocks" of information so that each focuses on one idea. Every sentence and detail in that paragraph should relate to and support that same idea. When your reader gets to the end of that paragraph she should know exactly what it was about.

Starting a new paragraph also signals to your reader that something new is about to come: another example, a change of scenery, or a new part of the story. Sometimes a transitional word can help your reader follow your train of thought; other times just starting a new paragraph will do the trick. You can arrange information within or between paragraphs in a number of ways: chronologically, by location or scene, in order of importance, or to build toward a conclusion or climax. Here are some examples:

Start to Finish

Ultimately, you want to create a compelling first sentence that hooks your reader and a well-written last sentence that nicely ties up your essay and leaves an impression. Everything you say in between should connect the two.

Chronological: In this essay, the author takes the reader through her travels, from early childhood through high school. We've only included the beginning of each paragraph to give you a sense of how the essay progresses.

In my life, I have taken many journeys without which I would not have experienced important truths. My father started us off early, taking us on many journeys to help us understand that true knowledge comes only from experience. We took trips every winter break to Madrid, Mexico, Costa Rica, and to Jamaica and Trinidad, my parents' homeland for Christmas . . . My truths were the truths of the tourist brochures: beautiful hotels, beaches, and cities . . .

I learned more about these truths in my sophomore year of high school, when I was among a group of students selected to visit Cuba . . .

My first impression of Cuba was . . .

The journeys I have taken have been colored by my prior experiences and by what my feelings were in those moments . . .

By location/scene: Here, the author starts by describing a memory driving with her father and then connects that moment to a memory of her with her brothers at home. Again, we've only included the beginning of these paragraphs.

My dad and I are driving down the winding South Carolina roads . . . I pull the sleeve of my sweatshirt over my hand and wipe a frosty layer off the glass so that I can see the passing trees. Our windshield wipers provide the only sound: an eerie rhythmic pumping. Eyes wide, I turn to my dad, a smile spreading across my face. "This is the perfect setting for a scary movie," I say, and I could not be happier.

My passion for videomaking sprouted from my longtime interest in scary movies. I've loved movies ever since I was five, when my sister and I would squeeze between our two older brothers for our weekend ritual: watching an episode of the Indiana Jones trilogy. . . .

Since then, my taste for "scary movies" has developed into an appreciation for many genres. I understand that anticipation can be created as much in a documentary as from a gigantic boulder rushing to crush our hero, but that initial kernel of excitement still remains.

Order of importance: The author starts by addressing his greatest concern over the Patriot Act and gradually works his way through examples that are most important to him.

Perhaps the most pressing issue concerning our country today is the Patriot Act, a bill passed by Congress shortly after the attacks of September 11, 2001 . . .

The policies that have been set into motion have come under heavy criticism from many Americans who claim that the Patriot Act infringes upon their constitutional rights . . .

While the Patriot Act has its shortcomings, it does contain some positive aspects, namely the taking down of the figurative walls constructed between different branches of government built during the Ford era as a result of Watergate . . .

Building toward a conclusion: The author starts by telling a story from his life in New York City; it is only at the end that we come to realize the connection these events have to his appreciation for the city's diversity.

I bounced my head to the music radiating from my earphones as I passed the platform for the shuttle train. The people around me were moving so fast that they created a blur of faces, heavy jackets, and quickly moving legs.

I noticed another man standing nearby. He was a middle-aged man who looked as if he had just stepped off the set of The Sopranos. After listening to the musician play a song, the man took his own guitar off his back and unzipped it. He placed the strap around his neck and gave the sitting musician a look that said, "Do you mind if I join you?" to which the elderly Asian man responded with a friendly, welcoming smile as he nodded his head. The two men began to play together . . .

Moments like this are what make us human beings. We aren't just individual entities concerned with only our own goals and not aware of the people around us. . . . I realized then that there were few other places in the world where such a diverse group of people could come together and all share the same bond. The bond of New Yorkers.

Topic Sentences

Think of the topic sentence as the "thesis statement" of each paragraph, which establishes that paragraph's main idea. The topic sentence needs to encompass all the points you want to discuss in that paragraph. Every sentence that follows the topic sentence serves as evidence to support the main point of that paragraph.

Occasionally a topic sentence can go at the end of the paragraph, to emphasize your point, but, in general, it works best as the first sentence in the paragraph, as in the following example:

> *I realize in retrospect that the process I went through in adjusting to the divorce*
> *analogous to the five stages Elisabeth Kübler-Ross writes about in* On Death
> Dying: *denial, anger, bargaining, depression, and acceptance.*

Introduction

In an academic essay, the thesis statement is usually the first or second sentence. However, when you are writing your college application essay, you can choose to organize and develop your ideas in more creative ways. For example, instead of starting with a thesis statement, you can start with an anecdote. Instead of writing, *Taking karate lessons taught me the importance of patience and humility,* consider hooking your reader by describing a scene in which you are practicing. This is what newspaper writers call a *lead.* A lead should orient your reader and get her excited to read your piece.

First Sentences

As we mentioned in the previous chapter, chances are you will probably delete your first sentence. As one New York City high school English teacher explains: "Often a kid comes to me with a draft. It reads 'blah, blah, blah,

blah, blah, blah, blah, blah, blah, blah, blah, blah, blah.' Then somewhere near the middle or end there's a terrific sentence. I say, 'Oh, good, *that's* your first sentence.' And I tell him to cross out everything else before it."

This is common. For many writers, their ideas form more fully and their writing comes to life only after they've started writing. This process is called *writing into it.*

Your challenge is to step back and look at your earlier drafts to find a compelling and unusual opening. You may need someone else to help you identify that great opener buried somewhere in your essay. Or, with a little distance, perhaps you can find it yourself.

You should really *like* your first sentences. If you don't, your reader won't either. Remember, you want to make a good first impression.

The first few sentences should be clear and should have a hook. Intrigue your reader. If your reader wonders "Why?" after your opener, you probably have a good lead.

Your first sentences should orient your reader. Make it clear where you are, what you are doing, and whether it's a past, present, or future event.

Your first sentences should be attention-grabbers: something that points to the significance of your topic. Here's an example of a compelling opening:

> According to Mother Teresa, "If you judge someone, you have no time to love them." I first saw this quote when it was posted on my sixth-grade classroom wall, and I hated it.

Background

After hooking your reader with your first sentence or two, you'll need to include facts that will help your reader understand the context of the situation you just described.

You need to include just enough background so it's clear—where you are, who else is there, what you are doing, and why. Don't overwhelm your reader with too many details. Remember, the admissions officer does not

"Think about when you're reading a book. You'd feel disappointed if you'd been sitting on the edge of your chair and you couldn't put it down, and then you got to the last chapter and it wasn't satisfying."

Gary Ross
Dean of Admissions,
Colgate University

INTRODUCTION Tips

1

Make an interesting observation.

2

Start in the middle of a scene, with an action.

3

Be concise.

4

Provide direction.

5

Be original.

6

Grab the reader's attention.

7

Make a confession.

8

Don't excessively set up the scene.

9

Give a glimpse of the main idea.

10

Set the tone for the rest of the essay.

want to read everything that has happened to you since you learned how to walk. Here's an example of including just enough details to make the picture clear:

> I feel sick. I'm nervous and my stomach's turning. The room is lined with neat rows of desks, each one occupied by another kid my age. We're all about to take the SATs. The proctor has instructed us to fill out section four: "race."

Avoid Clichéd Intros

A thousand essays begin with the horror and dread of waking up. Everyone wakes up in the morning—there is nothing interesting or unusual about it. Consider starting with an image of you doing something that has an implied action, so the reader wonders "Why?" For example, let's say you start by saying that you were standing on a bridge with a rock in your hand. That's interesting because the reader will wonder "Why does he have that rock in his hand? What is going to happen next?"

Provide Direction

In your introduction, you should give your reader clues about the content and theme of your essay so she knows what you're trying to convey and can prepare to follow you as you make your case. Provide direction without announcing it. Don't talk about what you are going to do in the essay: just do it, as in this example:

> I cannot be placed neatly into a single racial category, although I'm sure that people walking down the street don't hesitate to label me "caucasian." Never in my life has a stranger not been surprised when I told them I was half black.

Transitions

You don't necessarily need actual transitional words, because when a reader starts a new paragraph she is already assuming some kind of transition. Using action or narrative to make a transition can be as strong or stronger than using *on the other hand, moreover,* or *however.*

CONCLUSION
Tips

1

Don't repeat the same points.

2

Tie up loose ends.

3

Don't summaraize.

4

Don't introduce new topics.

5

Leave a strong impression.

6

Match the rest of the essay in tone and content.

7

Expand to broader context.

8

Keep it brief.

9

Make your strongest point.

10

Create a feeling of completion.

Conclusion

You want to leave a lasting impression on your reader. The conclusion, of course, is your last chance to do just that.

Your conclusion must relate to your main point. The end has to be true to the beginning. Don't introduce a new topic in the conclusion. You can, however, save a surprising or powerful nugget for the end.

Don't drag your reader through salutary phases such as *in summation* or *therefore*. You risk insulting your reader if you announce what you just said in the essay.

Starting All Over Again

Hearkening back to the introduction in your conclusion can be effective. For example, if you started with an anecdote, consider ending with a different part of the same story. Think of when you're watching a movie and you can tell it is about to end because suddenly you are at the same café, dinner table, or airplane scene where the movie began two hours ago. Look at this example:

> *At this point I realized that I had to be home soon and thanked him profusely for his generosity in answering my questions. As we walked toward the door, I noticed that I had left my hat on the table. I turned back to retrieve it, but by the time I had reached the doorway again, Che Guevara had disappeared into the mix of afternoon sunlight and shadow cast by the "El" tracks, as mysteriously as he had come.*

Ending Gracefully

The conclusion needs to complete the thought you've developed. But take care not to restate all your points again. Don't say, "In this essay I've explored and shown X, Y, and Z." If you need to announce the points you were trying to make in the essay, it means you didn't make the point clear enough in the body of your essay.

The Ripple Effect

If you don't have a conclusion, the last point you make will take on more weight than it deserves. Addressing a broader concept in the conclusion keeps your last point in perspective.

Take your ideas further. What are the broader implications of your main point? Your thesis probably describes the topic's significance to your immediate life. Expand upon your original thesis to explore what this means to your future, to your community, or perhaps even apply it universally. Here's an example:

> Through census forms, racial questionnaires on the SATs, and other devices, our society tries to draw conclusions about people based on appearance. It is a quick and easy way to categorize people without taking the time to get to know them, but it simply cannot be done.

7

STANDING OUT

"Unlike a novel, where you have a few hundred pages to get into a topic and get the excitement going, the essay only affords you a few hundred words. Action words and descriptions of action make it lively and grab the reader."

Brad Ward
Associate Director of Admissions,
Bucknell University

Visualize your essay. It's one or two pieces of paper stuck inside a file with a stack of other papers containing mostly numbers, scores, and grades. You want this particular document to grab the admissions officers and provide a brief, but memorable, experience.

You want to craft a lively, energetic, dynamic, and interesting piece of writing that offers your reader a window into your life.

Show, Don't Tell

"The more specific your essay is in terms of content, the more specific the approach to what you are talking about, the more specific examples you include of who you are, and the more you can tie it into why you want to go to the specific school you're applying to—these things make all the difference in the world."

Richard DiFeliciantonio
Vice President
for Enrollment,
Ursinus College

You are more likely to believe something if you've seen it with your own eyes than if you've heard about it secondhand. If someone told you that a 450-pound white tiger had escaped from a circus and was strolling through rush-hour traffic, you might not believe it. But if you were sitting in traffic and the tiger ambled in front of your car, you wouldn't need anyone to tell you there was a tiger loose on the highway.

We're not suggesting you include a videotape with your application. We are talking about creating what Gary Ross, Dean of Admissions at Colgate University, describes as a "word picture of something or someone that is important to you." Who are you more likely to believe: someone who says to you, "I am a trustworthy person," or someone who describes several situations that illustrate his trustworthiness? You can create a "word picture" through specific examples, details, and dialogue.

Be Specific

Admissions officers read thousands of essays a year, and most of them have been reading thousands of essays every year for many years. There is nothing general you can tell them that they haven't heard before. The more specific you are in your essay, the more you will stand out, because you will be telling them something that only you can tell. Other students may have had similar experiences but not in exactly the same way as you.

"You may be editor-in-chief of your student newspaper, but let's face it, we'll see thousands of essays by students who are editors-in-chief of their school newspapers," says Eric Furda, Former Director of Undergraduate Admissions at Columbia University. "That doesn't take away the honor of your post, but being editor-in-chief in itself isn't going to be unique. To make it more beneficial to you, you need to dig deeper and think about what being editor-in-chief is like. Explore what it was like to edit your friend's work or tough decisions you have had to make, like whether to put something in the paper in the name of freedom of speech even though you believe it overstepped the boundaries of civil discourse."

Use an Anecdote

An anecdote can demonstrate your point more powerfully than a statement. Telling a personal story that supports your thesis is an entertaining and effective way to give your readers a glimpse into your world while also strengthening your argument. The details you include reveal your personality, your values, and how you think. Here is an example of how you can use a personal anecdote in your essay:

> The stiff black apron hung awkwardly on my hips as I casually tried to tie the strings around my waist. I had been at Gino's Restaurant for only ten minutes when Maurizio, the manager, grabbed my arm abruptly and said, "Follow me to the dungeon." Unsure of whether he was joking, I smiled eagerly at him, but his glare confirmed his intent. I wiped the smirk off my face and followed him through the kitchen, which was louder than Madison Square Garden during a Knicks/Pacers game. A tall woman with a thick Italian accent pushed me while barking, "Move it, kid, you're blocking traffic." I later learned she was a waitress, and waitresses did not associate with the low-level busboys. Maurizio brought me to a dangerously steep staircase that looked like it had been purposely drenched in oil to increase the chance of a fall. As he gracefully flew down each step, I clutched onto the rusty tile walls, strategically putting one foot first and then the other. Eventually, I entered the "dungeon," and was directed to a table to join two men who were vigorously folding napkins.

Set a Scene

Your choice of small details also creates atmosphere. For example, rather than coming right out and stating that reaching the peak of a particularly challenging mountain was the coolest thing you've ever done, try to get that same feeling across to the reader by talking about the wonder and sense of accomplishment you felt when you reached the top. But stating it in abstract terms will not create a sense of awe. Evoke an image through details of your hike. Show the reader what made that hike special—the lighting, the sounds, the weather, the blend of colors, the smell of the air—and you will make her feel how you felt.

Be as detailed and specific as possible. Instead of leaving your reader with a fuzzy image, leave her with a scene she won't be able to forget. Make her feel like she was there. Instead of writing, *I am a disciplined clarinet player, dedicated to practicing every day,* paint a scene with the details. Describe the callus you have on the back of your right thumb from holding the clarinet for hours every day, the feel of the wood in your hands, the sound the case makes when you open it and pull the clarinet out of the velvet lining, the woody taste of the reed in your mouth. Your reader will sense your connection to the clarinet and feel as if she has gone through your daily practice routine with you.

> **Abstract/Nondescript:** *I felt awe and wonder as I climbed to the top of the mountain.*
>
> **Concrete/Detailed:** *I fell into a meditative trance as I took each step. The trees had turned bright gold and were glistening in the sun, and I was increasingly aware of how connected I felt to the world with each step I took.*

When you describe a situation in detail, the reader can sense what you want them to feel so you don't need to say, "I felt sad." Talk about the golf ball–sized lump in your throat when your mom told you that the family was moving across the country right before your senior year of high school. Your reader will get a better sense of how you were feeling if you explore how you felt and describe it, rather than state it.

Elicit Emotion

The only way for your emotions to rub off on the reader is for you to be connected to the topic or the mood you are trying to convey. As we said in Chapter 2, the topic you choose needs to be important to you. That way, you will be emotionally connected to your topic and your reader will pick up on that. "Always write about something important to you. That's a basic tenet to writing," says Richard DiFeliciantonio, Vice President for Enrollment at Ursinus College.

"No tears in the writer, no tears in the reader."

Robert Frost

Choose Your Details

So far, we've talked about the importance of peppering your prose with details. Significant details make your words leap off the page and find their way into the admissions officer's head—and maybe even her heart. But, at the same time, you don't want to cram every single detail you can think of into every sentence of your essay. You need to pick and choose your details with care.

For starters, the essay has a word limit. Additionally, too many details will distract the reader from your argument. If sentence after sentence is thick with details, the reader won't know which details are most important and will find it challenging to follow the action or your line of thought. You don't want to make your reader work hard to figure out what you are saying.

To find the right balance, decide which details are the most unusual and interesting and which really reveal something about your personality or the situation you are

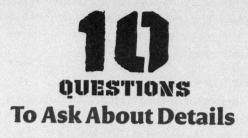

QUESTIONS
To Ask About Details

1

What is the point of including this detail?

2

Is it appropriate?

3

Is it interesting?

4

Is it unusual?

5

Does it reveal something about my personality?

6

Does it clarify the situation I'm describing?

7

Does it enhance the mood I'm trying to convey?

8

Does it support the main idea of my essay?

9

Does it follow the action of my essay?

10

Will the reader understand why I included it?

describing. Think about which details enhance your essay and strongly support what you are trying to say.

> **Too many details:** *I can still remember the day vividly, although it was twelve years and three months ago. It was autumn in suburban Chicago and I was in the ballet studio at the Winnetka Community House, dressed in an aquamarine leotard (the color that all children in the Ballet for Beginners class were required to wear), pink tights, pink leather ballet shoes, and my long dark brown hair was falling out of the bobby pins in the bun which I had begged my mother to make so I would "look like a real ballerina."*

> **Just the right amount of detail:** *I can still remember the day vividly, although it was twelve years ago. I was dressed in an aquamarine leotard and pink tights, and my hair was falling out of the bun I had begged my mother to make so I would "look like a real ballerina."*

Use All Five Senses

Details about the way something looks, smells, tastes, sounds, or feels make whatever it is you're describing seem more real to the reader. The essay is supposed to present a piece of your world to the admissions officer. Close your eyes and imagine a scene from your past for a few moments. When you open your eyes, ask yourself:

1. Where was I?
2. What were some memorable physical characteristics of the person I am describing?
3. What sounds, smells, or textures do I remember?
4. What did people say?
5. Was I eating? If so, what?
6. What was I wearing? Was it that sweater Grandma knit that always makes my neck itch?
7. Was I cold?
8. Was I embarrassed?
9. Was I scared?
10. Was I nervous?

Here's an example of just the right amount of detail: We met for lunch at El Burrito Mexicano, a tiny Mexican lunch counter under the Red Line "El" tracks. I arrived first and took a seat, facing the door. Behind me the TV showed highlights from the Mexican Soccer League. I felt nervous and unsure. How would I be received by a famous revolutionary—an upper middle-class American kid asking a Communist hero questions? Then I spotted him in the doorway and my breath caught in my throat. In his overcoat, beard, and beret, he looked as if he had just stepped out from one of Batista's "wanted" posters. I rose to greet Ernesto "Che" Guevara and we shook hands. At the counter we ordered: he, enchiladas verdes and a beer, and I, a burrito and two "limonadas." The food arrived and we began to talk.

Concrete examples are more compelling to your reader than abstract concepts. Don't try to attack an issue, such as injustice, without a specific example. The way to make an issue hit home is to put a face to it. For example, if you are writing about injustice, don't just say that injustice makes you mad. Describe shopping with an African-American friend and noticing how he was followed around the store because of his skin color; explore how that made you feel and how the experience opened your eyes and made you want to take action.

Use Strong Verbs and Nouns

Be as specific as possible with your verbs and nouns. Instead of writing, *I went to the park*, think about how you went. Did you walk? If so, how? In a determined manner, or did you take your time? Did you drive? In what kind of car? How fast?

Instead of using adverbs (*I walked home slowly*) to describe an action, think of a verb that might more specifically describe how you walked (*I slouched home*).

Similarly, with nouns you should always favor the specific over the general. Don't write, *I was eating a bland dinner*. Write, *I swallowed another bite of my tuna casserole*. Rely more on nouns and verbs than adjectives and adverbs.

Stay on Message

One surefire way to lose your reader is to talk about stuff that has nothing to do with your thesis. If you are writing about your parents' divorce, don't go on a tangent and discuss your favorite band. As we discussed in

Chapter 6, each topic sentence should relate to your thesis, and every sentence following your topic sentence should further your argument.

Clarity

You also risk losing your reader's interest when your writing becomes vague. Reread your essay and ask yourself, could someone who doesn't know me and isn't familiar with the situation understand what is going on? Do you have a sentence that is so long and tortured that your reader will need to reread it three times before having any idea of what you are trying to say? Can your reader tell to whom your pronouns refer? If you started with a flashback and then shifted to the present, will the reader be able to follow?

Word Choice

When choosing words, go for variety and impact. Don't repeat the same words throughout your essay, and try not to use words that have been overused so much that they barely mean anything anymore. For example, take a look at the following excerpt:

> I saw quite a beautiful sunset the other day. It was amazing and it brought tears to my eyes. It had a big impact on me. I am really amazed by the beauty of our natural surroundings. We have a responsibility as citizens of the earth to preserve the beauty of nature.

Avoid qualifiers like *very*, *little*, and *rather*. These "are the leeches that infest the pond of prose, sucking the blood of words," write William Strunk, Jr., and E. B. White in *The Elements of Style*.

Meghan Cadwallader, Assistant Director of Admissions at Susquehanna University, offers these words of advice:

Adjectives

When you have an adjective that tells, exchange it for a verb that shows. Instead of writing *angry cat*, write *Henrietta hissed*. Instead of *scary storm*, write *the sky lit up and the storm howled*.

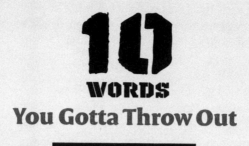

10

WORDS
You Gotta Throw Out

We asked English teachers and admissions officers to list some of their
least favorite words. Here's what they came up with:

1
Very

2
A lot

3
Really

4
Cool

5
Amazing

6
Wonderful

7
Basically

8
Definitely

9
Deal with it (as in the verb, to deal with something)

10
Hopefully

"Certain words recur in essays no matter what the essays are about—words like *responsibility* and *commitment*, or *maturity*. These are positive words but don't really tell me anything. They're very vague. Be as specific as possible."

Clichés

Like words, expressions can be overused. Look carefully to see if you include any clichéd sayings in your essay, such as "American as apple pie."

If you use a famous quote in your essay, consider finding one that is less well-known. Even if your essay is thoughtful and sound, your essay won't stand out from the crowd if dozens of other applicants use the same quote.

Fresh, original language and ideas show you have imagination; worn-out words, sayings, and quotations have a numbing effect on the reader. After a certain point, words and sayings that have been said billions of times mean nothing at all.

"There is a fine line between appropriate and conservative, and a flat-out cliché, which can be tiresome," says Richard DiFeliciantonio. "It's not necessarily fatal, but your essay is not doing as much good as it could be doing."

Easy on the Eyes

The college application essay is not all about content. On a superficial level, looks count. If you use ultrasmall font and your sentences and paragraphs are long, your essay will look like a wall of text on the page. Make it *look* like an energetic essay.

For roughly six weeks, admissions officers do nothing but read files for forty hours a week. If they are confronted with something physically imposing, or if they pick up an essay and it is a block of miniscule print, you will instill them with dread even before they start reading.

This is not the time to become James Joyce. The megaparagraph is deadly. Alter paragraph length. When you can, aim for shorter, punchier paragraphs like the ones you see in newspapers or sports magazines. This helps make the page look more user-friendly for the reader. It will certainly be more digestible. Think of how you would feel: would you prefer to read six or seven short paragraphs or three really long ones?

CLICHÉS
To Avoid

1

What goes around comes around.

2

Live and learn.

3

Good things come to those who wait.

4

There's no such thing as a free ride.

5

When life gives you lemons, make lemonade.

6

If you can't beat them, join them.

7

Beauty is only skin deep.

8

You can't judge a book by its cover.

9

No pain, no gain.

10

When it rains, it pours.

The bottom line on standing out is this: your essay should be as unique as you are. If you infuse your writing with originality and paint an honest picture of yourself, the admissions committee will likely remember your essay and realize what a valuable addition you would be to their academic community.

10

Formatting Tips

1

Use a standard typeface, like Times, Arial, or Courier.

2

Use a point size between 10 and 12.

3

Use one-inch margins.

4

Left-justify your paragraphs.

5

Double-space, unless you're limited to one page.

6

Print in black font.

7

Indent paragraphs.

8

Avoid bolding or underlining words.

9

Use italics sparingly.

10

Avoid symbols like smiley faces.

GRAMMAR & PUNCTUATION

"We expect people to approach the essay as if they were already students at Colgate and this is a required class assignment. If we get the sense that someone is careless or has no grasp of grammar, we view it as merely a foreshadowing of how this person is going to approach work in the classroom. No matter how compelling the story, we're not going to look past the fact that this person didn't take the assignment seriously."

Gary Ross
Dean of Admissions,
Colgate University

Admissions officers will evaluate your potential based on the ideas you present, as well as the tone and style you employ. They want to know that you can write well. If your essay is riddled with grammatical mistakes, they will either think that you missed some important elementary school lessons or that you're just plain careless.

Don't worry: we're not going to bore you with all the rules of grammar. By your senior year of high school, you should have a basic grasp of the English language. If you read your essay aloud enough times, you can probably catch most of your mistakes just by listening to how the sentences sound.

In this chapter we focus on the ten most common writing errors made in application essays. We've also included a crash course in grammar at the end of the chapter.

Error #1

Verb Tense

Is your essay in the present tense or in past tense? Do you shift back and forth between the two tenses without rhyme or reason?

It's a common mistake to start off in the present tense, drift into the past, then drift back to the present, without even realizing that you're doing it. Shifting verb tenses will make you seem like a less reliable narrator. If you're going to switch tenses, make sure you do it correctly.

> **Inappropriate tense shift:** I *turn* on the radio and hit the gas, *back* out of my driveway, and *head* down my street, thinking with excitement about what it will be like to meet my grandfather for the first time. When I *got* to O'Hare Airport, I *started* to get nervous.

"Colleges place a premium on strong writing skills. We look for a mastery of the mechanics of writing as well as fluency and originality. The essay illustrates your readiness for college writing classes."

Richard DiFeliciantonio Vice President for Enrollment, Ursinus College

In this example, there is no reason to suddenly switch to the past tense in the last sentence. It's OK to recount a past experience using the present tense, but you have to stick with it.

> **Effective tense shift:** *I often **think** about the drive to O'Hare to meet my grandfather for the first time. As I **pulled** out of my driveway and **got** onto the expressway, I **was** excited and nervous, but I **had** no idea how much my life was about to change. Today, my views of the world **are** colored by the lessons my grandfather **taught** me.*

In this example, a past event is used to reflect upon the narrator's present views; the tense switches enrich the writing.

When discussing a work of literature, use the present tense to talk about the events that take place in the novel. When talking about your experience reading it, use the past tense:

> *The first time I **read** The Great Gatsby, I **related** to Nick Caraway, an isolated dreamer who **is** trapped in a demanding reality.*

Another common tense mistake is using the past perfect (*had*, plus the past tense of a verb) for no good reason. Don't write **I had eaten dinner** if what you really mean to say is *I ate dinner*. Use the past perfect when you want to show that an event that took place in the past occurred before another past event. For example:

> *I **had eaten** dinner by the time my mother **arrived** home that night.*

Use the present perfect to show a link between past and present. This tense shows you still do something as opposed to the action being completely in the past. For example:

> *I **have played** soccer all my life.*

If you want to show that an event or behavior came to end, stick with the past tense:

> *I **played** soccer all my life, until my mother **fell** ill.*

Error #2

Subject/Verb Agreement

A singular subject (such as *puppy*) requires a singular verb (*plays*); a plural subject (*puppies*) requires a plural verb (*play*). This is pretty easy, but it can get confusing when your subject is a collective noun (such as *family, group, team,* or *class*). A collective noun implies more than one person but is considered singular and takes a singular verb:

> The **family hopes** to find a house by the ocean.

Certain things that go together seem plural but are actually singular:

> **Peanut butter and jelly is** my favorite sandwich.

Also, the words *each, either, neither, everyone, nobody, somebody,* and *no one* are singular and require a singular verb:

> **Nobody likes** learning the rules of grammar.

Error #3

Active vs. Passive Voice

When you revise your writing, ask yourself this: who is performing the action? If you can't answer this question, then chances are you are using the passive voice. Take a look at this sentence:

> The citizens were not informed of the looming danger.

From this sentence, we know that the citizens weren't informed, but we don't know who failed to inform them. To turn a passive sentence into an active one, you need to name names and assign responsibility:

> **The police** did not inform the citizens of the looming danger.

Use the active voice instead of the passive voice whenever possible. The passive voice will make your writing dull and listless; the active voice, which allows you to use strong, interesting verbs, will make your writing lively and energetic.

Look at your verbs: is the subject acting or being acted upon? Giving or receiving? Rewrite your sentences after you've figured out who's doing the action, and insert the doer into the sentence.

Passive: *I was given a drum set for my third birthday.*

Active: *My favorite aunt gave me a drum set for my third birthday.*

Passive: *Thanksgiving dinner was eaten in silence.*

Active: *We ate Thanksgiving dinner in silence.*

Error #4
Commonly Misused Words

There are countless words that students confuse and misuse in their writing. These errors aren't fatal, but they'll make your writing look sloppy. Here are the top 10:

1. It's vs. Its

It's is a contraction, meaning "it is." *Its* is a possessive pronoun *(The television series is in **its** final season).* Possessive pronouns *(his, hers, whose, its, ours, theirs, and yours)* do not take apostrophes.

Use contractions like *it's* sparingly in your writing. Some admissions officers perceive contractions as too informal for an application essay.

2. Affect vs. Effect

Affect is a verb, meaning "to influence":

*The death of my grandmother **affected** me deeply.*

The word *affect* can also be used as a noun, but you will pretty much never use it (at least not in your application essay) unless you become a social psychologist.

Effect can be a verb or a noun. As a noun, it means "result." As a verb, it means "to bring about":

*The presidential debates had an **effect** on the outcome of the election.*

*As president of student council, I **effected** significant change.*

3. **Appraise vs. Apprise**

To *appraise* is to figure out the value of something:

> After **appraising** the drawing, Richard informed Cynthia that her art was worthless.

To *apprise* is to give someone information:

> In an urgent undertone, Donald **apprised** me of the worrisome situation.

4. **Desert vs. Dessert**

A *desert* is a place with sand and camels:

> The cartoon character pulled himself across the **desert**, calling out for water.

A *dessert* is something sweet that you eat after a meal:

> My favorite **dessert** is cookie-dough ice cream.

5. **Lose vs. Loose**

To *lose* something is to misplace it or shake it off:

> Michael tried to **lose** the hideous shirt his girlfriend had given him for Christmas.

Loose means "movable," "unfastened," or "promiscuous":

> The **loose** chair leg snapped off, and Doug fell to the floor.

6. **Principal vs. Principle**

The *principal* is the person who calls the shots in your high school:

> **Principal** Skinner rules Springfield Elementary School with an iron fist, yet he still lives with his mother.

A *principle* is a value or standard.

> Edward, a boy of **principle**, refused to cheat on the test.

7. **Eminent vs. Imminent**

An *eminent* person is one who is well known and highly regarded:

> The **eminent** author disguised herself with a beret and dark glasses.

An *imminent* event is one that is just about to happen:

> When the paparazzi's arrival seemed **imminent**, the celebrities ducked out the back entrance.

8. Lie vs. Lay

People often confuse these two. To *lie* is an intransitive verb; it describes an action being performed by something or someone. To *lay* is a transitive verb; it describes an action that needs to be done to something. The tricky thing to remember is that *lay* is also the past tense of the verb *lie*:

Lie (lay, lain, lying)

Present tense: *I lie down on my towel and soak up the sun.*

Past tense: *I lay down on my towel and soaked up the sun.*

Lay (laid, laid, laying)

Present tense: *I lay the pencil on the desk and try to focus on the question.*

Past tense: *I laid the pencil on the desk and tried to focus on the question.*

9. However

Don't start a sentence with *however*. When placed at the beginning of a sentence, *however* means "in whatever way," not "but":

However she decides to get to school, I hope she gets there on time.

It is, however, OK to insert *however* in the middle of a sentence:

*I don't care how she gets to school. I do, **however**, hope she gets to school on time.*

Another option is to start your sentence with *but* rather than *however*:

But she is in danger of arriving late if she drives to school.

10. Very Unique

Unique means "without like or equal." There are no degrees of uniqueness; if something is unique, it is one of a kind.

Incorrect: *My cousin has a **very unique** personality.*

Correct: *My cousin has a **unique** personality.*

Error #5
Ambiguous Pronouns

Writing is about communicating. Don't make your reader guess the meaning of a pronoun. It should always be clear who *it, they, she, he, him,* or *her* is.

> **Ambiguous:** *My dad met with the coach, and* **he** *told* **him** *that I was having health problems.*

Who is *he*? Who is *him*? Instead, write:

> **Clear:** *My dad met with the coach, and he told the coach that I was having health problems.*

Error #6
Sentence Structure and Variety

The subject/verb sentence construction dominates most writing (*I ate, We sang, The bird chirped*). In order to avoid boring your readers to death, vary your sentence structure.

> **Undesirable:** *Her husband does not allow her to work. He does not allow her to take care of her baby. She longs to do something other than rest. Everyone says she is sick and must relax. She is trapped in her room. She begins to go mad.*

> **Better:** *Because of her purported illness, everyone, including her husband, insists she must rest instead of working or taking care of her baby. Trapped in her room, she begins to go mad.*

By varying your sentence structure, you not only keep things lively, but also you indicate to your readers which assertions are most important. They'll instinctively understand that subordinated details (*trapped in her room*) aren't as crucial as prominent points (*she begins to go mad*), and they'll have a much easier time understanding your writing.

Also vary the length of your sentences. A varied rhythm to your words keeps your reader awake.

Error #7
Wordiness

With only 500 words to get your point across, you want to be as concise as possible. Being wordy means failing to use only the words you absolutely need. If you see phrases like *being that* or *in regard to the fact that* or even just *the fact that* in your writing, you've fallen prey to wordiness. Here are some easy ways to keep your writing brief:

Avoid Unnecessary Definitions

Don't waste precious space explaining the obvious:

> We rushed to the emergency room, a bleak place where people who are sick or who have been in an accident wait until a doctor can see them.

There's no need to define "emergency room," as it speaks for itself:

> We rushed to the emergency room.

It is and *There are*

Avoid starting a sentence with *It is* or *There are*:

Wordy: *It is my father who makes the decisions in my house.*

Better: *My father makes the decisions in my house.*

Wordy: *There are some people who just don't know when to stop writing.*

Better: *Some people just don't know when to stop writing.*

Wordy: *It is to be expected that admissions officers care about grammar.*

Better: *Admissions officers are expected to care about grammar.*

Wordy: *There are many high school seniors who worry about getting into college.*

Fix: *Many high school seniors worry about getting into college.*

10

Redundant Phrases

1
Close proximity

2
End result

3
Mutual cooperation

4
Past history

5
True facts

6
Being homesick

7
Usual customs

8
Divide up

9
Protest against

10
Cooperate together

Personally **and** *I think*

You can leave out *personally* and *I think,* because the reader knows the words on the paper are your beliefs:

> **Wordy:** *Personally, I think the Patriot Act provides the government with abusive police powers and methods to invade our privacy.*

> **Wordy:** *I think the Patriot Act provides the government with abusive police powers and methods to invade our privacy.*

> **Better:** *The Patriot Act provides the government with abusive police powers and methods to invade our privacy.*

Two Words Are Not Better Than One

Don't use two words to say the same thing:

> *I was **happy** and **thrilled** when my uncle told me he was visiting.*

Choose the stronger word and delete the other. Similarly, you may have two sentences that say pretty much the same thing, just in slightly different ways. It's tempting to use both, but decide which one is stronger and cut the other.

Error #8
Parallelism

In every sentence, all of the different components must start, continue, and end in the same, or *parallel,* way. It's especially common to find errors of parallelism in sentences that list actions or items. For example:

> *In the pool area, there is **no spitting, no running,** and **don't toss** your half-eaten candy bars in the water.*

The first two forbidden pool activities end in *-ing* (*-ing* words are called gerunds), and because of that, the third forbidden must also end in *-ing.* If you start with gerunds, you must continue with gerunds all the way through a list:

> *In the pool area, there is **no spitting, no running,** and **no tossing** of half-eaten candy bars in the water.*

Error #9:

Punctuation

Using punctuation correctly is vital to ensuring your essay is an effective piece of writing. Misusing commas, semicolons, and other punctuation marks can seriously hurt the impression you make on the admissions officers, and it can even make parts of your essay unintelligible.

Although a few minor errors may not make a huge difference to your reader, only error-free application essays can be considered truly outstanding. You should know the basics, as listed here:

Commas

When you join two complete sentences with conjunctions, such as *and, but,* or *for,* place a comma before the conjunction:

> *I want to go, but it is snowing.*

If you're unsure whether you need a comma, check to see if the subject changes over the course of the sentence. If it does, you need a comma:

> *The parrot squawks obscenities, and the dog eats nothing but steak.*

If there is no subject following the conjunction, you don't need a comma:

> *The parrot squawks obscenities and eats nothing but crackers.*

Do not join independent clauses with a comma. Instead, use a period or a semicolon:

> **Incorrect:** *It is about to snow, we'd better not go.*

> **Correct:** *It is about to snow; we'd better not go.*

> **Correct:** *It is about to snow. We'd better not go.*

Be sure to enclose parenthetical statements in commas:

> *My father, an avid skier, wants to move to Colorado.*

Also use a comma to separate parts of a date or an address:

> *My niece was born in Morristown, New Jersey, on May 24, 2002.*

Finally, be sure to separate items in a list with commas:

> **Incorrect:** *Chocolate pizza pasta and ice cream are my favorite foods.*

> **Correct:** *Chocolate, pizza, pasta and ice cream are my favorite foods.*

Colons and Semicolons

"Don't throw in colons or semicolons if you don't know how to use them," warns Meghan Cadwallader, Assistant Director of Admissions at Susquehanna University. "Sometimes students try to throw in some hefty punctuation. They think, 'I'm going to use a colon now: watch out.' It all goes back to using things properly."

The semicolon indicates a pause. It is stronger than a comma but weaker than a period:

My father has a wonderful sense of humor; nevertheless, he is a strict man.

The colon means "as follows":

The five stages of grief are: denial, anger, bargaining, depression, and acceptance.

It should not be used to introduce a short list:

Incorrect: *I went to the store and picked up: corn on the cob, hamburger meat, and beefsteak tomatoes.*

Correct: *I went to the store and picked up corn on the cob, hamburger meat, and beefsteak tomatoes.*

A colon can also be used to introduce a single word or phrase, to show a close connection between the two parts, or to add dramatic effect.

There was only one problem with her theory: she had no proof.

Quotation Marks

Commas and periods always go inside the closing quotation mark:

"I ate too much," said my little brother.

My little brother said, "I ate too much."

The first word of a quotation is capitalized, but if you interrupt the quote, don't capitalize the first word of the continuation:

"Because of your rude behavior," said Mr. Littell, "you can't come on the class field trip."

Exclamation Marks

Do not use exclamation marks to strengthen weak words. The exclamation mark should only be used for true exclamations or for commands (and never use more than one):

What a day!

Stop!

Error #10

Spelling

Relying heavily on word-processing programs like SpellCheck or Grammar-Check can get you into trouble by lulling you into a false sense of security. For example, SpellCheck doesn't detect if you use the wrong word; it only notices if a word is spelled incorrectly. So if you're not careful, it's easy to miss that you wrote the word compete when you meant to write complete.

Incorrect: *I completed in twenty three gymnastics meats last year.*

Correct: *I competed in twenty-three gymnastics meets last year.*

If you're lucky, the admissions officers will be able to guess from the context what you are trying to say. But there is no reason to look careless.

A Quick Crash Course in Grammar

We've broken the basics of language into five main sections: verbs, agreement, modifiers and modifications, clause organization, and usage.

Verbs

Good writing depends on actions and chronology—who did what to whom when? If you want to prevent your readers from getting lost, make sure you drive them in the right direction.

Past vs. Present Perfect

The **past** tense signifies that something occurred or existed in the past. It is indicated by an *–ed* at the end of a word, or by an equivalent irregular form, such as *flew* or *thought*:

> Barbara worked in New York long ago.

This means that Barbara worked in New York at some definite point in the past. She no longer works there.

The **present perfect** tense refers either to something that began in the past and continues into the present or something that occurred in the past but still has some bearing on the present. It is indicated by using *has/have* plus the *–ed* (or the equivalent irregular) form of a verb:

> Barbara has worked in New York before.

Unlike the previous sentence, this sentence means that Barbara worked in New York at some unspecified point in the past.

> Barbara has worked in New York for twenty years.

This sentence means that Barbara started working in New York at some point in the past, never stopped, and is still working there in the present.

There are a few words that signal that the present perfect rather than the past should be used. The table on the following page explains these **signpost** words.

Signpost Word	Example	Comment
ever	*Bill has read novels ever since he retired.*	Notice how this sentence uses both the present perfect and the past. *Bill has read novels* means that Bill started reading novels at some point in the past and still reads them in the present. *[E]ver since he retired* means that Bill started reading novels at a definite point in the past—when he retired.
never	*Evan has never been one to restrain himself.*	This means that at no point in the past—and up to the present moment—has Evan been able to control himself. A state of being began at some indefinite point in the past has continued up to the present moment.
since	*Since learning to swim, Ingmar has enjoyed the ocean.*	Again, an action has occurred at some indefinite point in the past and continues to this day.
yet	*The book hasn't been written yet.*	A particular state of being—that of not completing the book—has not occurred since some indefinite point in the past and continues not to occur up to the present moment.

Past vs. Past Perfect

The **past perfect** tense (also known as **pluperfect**) refers to something that began and ended before something else occurred in the past. The past perfect tense is "more past than the past." It is indicated by using *had* plus the *–ed* (or equivalent irregular) form:

> *Darwin had visited the Cape de Verde Islands before he visited the Galapagos Islands.*

This means that Darwin's presence in the Cape de Verde Islands preceded his presence in the Galapagos Islands, which itself occurred in the past.

As a rule, if you have two actions that occurred in the past, put the one that occurred deeper in the past in the past perfect tense. The more recent action should be in the past tense.

If-clauses

What's the difference between the following two sentences?

> *If I really study this book, I will improve my essay-writing ability.*

> *If I were the president, I would do things a lot differently.*

The first sentence states that if a condition is fulfilled (*really studying this book*), then a particular action will result (*improving your essay-writing ability*). The second sentence states something that's contrary to fact, something imagined that exists only in thought. The person making that statement is not the president, clearly, but is projecting himself into that person's situation.

The first sentence is in the **indicative** mood; the second sentence is in the **subjunctive** mood. (Don't worry too much about the names used here.)

The main point is the form of the second (subjunctive) sentence. The if-clause should never include a *would* verb; *would* is used only in the second clause, which we'll call the would-clause:

> **Incorrect:** *If you would have stayed longer, you would have had more fun.*

> **Correct:** *If you had stayed longer, you would have had more fun.*

In the correct example, the if-clause is in the past perfect and the would-clause is in the present perfect.

Agreement

If words don't agree with one another in a sentence, meaning is obscured. Aside from subject/verb agreement, which we explained earlier, there are several types of agreement.

Intervening Clauses and Phrases

You're going to want to vary the sentence structure in your essay. However, you need to vary your sentences grammatically, but in such a way that doesn't obscure your meaning. So let's look at some more complex sentences with subject/verb agreement in mind.

> The prescription of antidepressants, which is driven by the fact that medications are more likely to be covered by insurance than psychotherapy, often lead to burying the sources of depression.

See the error? If not, get rid of the intervening clause:

> The prescription of antidepressants often lead to burying the sources of depression.

Can you see it now? If not, isolate the subject and verb:

> The <u>prescriptions of antidepressants</u> often <u>lead</u> to burying the sources of depression.
> **Subject**   **Verb**

Antidepressants is not the subject—the prescription of antidepressants is. Prescription is singular; lead is the plural form of the verb. You need the singular form of the verb to match the singular subject.

The correct version is:

> The prescription of antidepressants, which is driven by that fact that medications are more likely to be covered by insurance than psychotherapy, often leads to burying the sources of depression.

Hidden and Compound Subjects

Here's another typical error you may commit when you try to vary your sentence structure:

> Inside the tank is a goldfish and a snail.

Tricky! The subject is hidden here—it's not the tank. What if you flip the sentence around so that the subject, which we're accustomed to seeing at the beginning of a sentence, comes first?

> *A goldfish and a snail is inside the tank.*

The *is* sticks out more when the sentence is rewritten this way; it should be *are*. *A goldfish* and *a snail* is a compound subject; compound subjects take plural verbs. Only the word *and* can create a compound subject. *As well as, or,* and *along with* do not create compound subjects:

> *Rock and jazz are influential musical styles.*
> *Rock, as well as jazz, is an influential musical style.*
> *Rock, along with jazz, is an influential musical style.*
> *Rock or jazz is an influential musical style.*

Singular or Plural?

What's wrong with the following sentence?

> *Neither of those two musical styles are as influential as blues.*

The problem is that *neither, either,* and *none* take singular, not plural, verbs. The correction is:

> *Neither of those two musical styles is as influential as blues.*

Finally, watch out for nouns that seem plural but are actually singular, such as:

> *The series of plays was very entertaining.*
> *The team was crushed by the loss.*
> *The couple finds life together to be challenging.*

Series, team, and *couple* are singular nouns that refer to groups. *Group,* actually, is another good example. By definition, a group has more than one member, but a group itself is singular: one group; many groups.

Noun/Number Agreement

> *All people enjoy maintaining their yard.*

You might think this sentence is OK, but it's incorrect. As written, it means that every single person currently alive, as well as all persons that have ever lived, enjoy maintaining the one yard they've all shared! That's a big yard.

Nouns have to agree in number—start with plural, end with plural; start with singular, end with singular. This sentence should be:

> *All people enjoy maintaining their yards.*

Here's another common mistake to avoid:

> *Bob, Jim, and Neil are planning to give up music in order to become a writer.*

How can three people, Bob, Jim, and Neil, become one writer? Well, they can't:

> *Bob, Jim, and Neil are planning to give up music in order to become writers.*

Countability

Another common error involving nouns is what we call **countability**. Look at the following sentences:

> *I have many disappointments.*

> *You would be wise to show less hatred toward others.*

Both sentences are correct. *Disappointments* are something one could count; *disappointments* are discrete entities like *puppies* or *galaxies* or *staplers*. *Hatred*, however, cannot be counted; *hatred* is an abstract state of being, as are *oppression, liberty,* and *apathy*. Concrete entities—*air* and *water*, to name two—can be noncountable as well. (*Putting on airs* and *parting the waters* are figuratively countable uses of these noncountable nouns.)

Countability is most often indicated via the less/fewer and number/amount pairings. Here's a handy chart:

Noun	Countable?	Use	Example
happiness	no	less	*Why aim for less happiness than you can achieve?*
virus	yes	fewer	*There are fewer viruses than bacteria.*
fear	no	less	*The less fear we feel, the better we are able to think.*
joke	yes	fewer	*If you told fewer jokes, the class could make more progress.*
computer	yes	number	*The number of home computers has skyrocketed in the past twenty years.*

Noun	Countable?	Use	Example
courage	no	amount	*The amount of courage a leader inspires is a telling measure of his value.*
flower	yes	number	*I have a number of flowers on my kitchen table.*
joy	no	amount	*The value of one's life is proportional to the amount of joy in it.*

Pronoun/Number Agreement

Did everyone forget to bring their raincoat with them?

The question above is grammatically incorrect.

Everyone is singular, strange as that may seem. You might think that everyone refers to a collection of people, but it refers to each individual in a collection of people—*everyone*.

To highlight this error, substitute the equivalent phrase *each of you* into the sentence:

Did each of you forget to bring their raincoat with them?

The pronoun *their* is plural, but it refers back to a singular subject, *each of you*—or, in the previous sentence, *everyone*. The proper form is:

Did everyone forget to bring his or her raincoat with him or her?

Yes, this is cumbersome, but correct.

The following words behave just like everyone: *anyone, no one, nobody, every, each.*

Check out this sentence:

Spacely Sprockets reported today that their workforce had accepted management's demands.

Sprockets may be plural, but presumably there is only one company called *Spacely Sprockets*. If it's a single company, it requires a singular pronoun:

*Spacely Sprockets reported today that **its** workforce had accepted management's demands.*

Pronoun Shift

Watch out for **pronoun shift** too:

Incorrect: *If you start with a particular pronoun, one shouldn't shift to another later on in the sentence.*

Correct: *If one would like to do as well as one can on the essay, one should keep this common error in mind.*

Correct: *That way, you will be happy with the essay you write.*

Ambiguous and Vague Pronouns

Ambiguous pronouns lack a clear antecedent; **vague pronouns** lack an antecedent altogether. **Antecedent** refers to the noun (or pronoun) that a pronoun refers to (*ante* meaning "before" in Latin).

In the following sentence, the pronoun is bolded:

Donna told Marie about her knitting.

Whose knitting are we talking about, Donna's or Marie's? They're both women, so it's impossible to tell. Replace *her* with either *Donna's* or *Marie's* and you've solved the problem:

Donna told Marie about Donna's knitting.

or

Donna told Marie about Marie's knitting.

Be on the lookout for all kinds of ambiguities. Look at the following sentence:

Mike gave his brother a bass amplifier that he used every chance he could get.

This seems less ambiguous, because we tend to interpret the sentence according to our experience and expectations: "Mike's a nice guy; he gave his brother a bass amp. That brother used that amp every chance he could get. How touching!"

That's all well and good, except that it is possible that Mike gave his brother a bass amp and that Mike, not his brother, used it every chance he got. Maybe Mike's a selfish brother. Maybe Mike's brother hated the amp. The point is, we've got an ambiguous pronoun (he), and that obscures meaning.

Now, what's wrong with the following sentence?

They say that global warming will only get worse.

On its own, the *they* in this sentence has no antecedent at all. There are many ways to rewrite this sentence; here's one option:

A panel of expert climatologists says that global warming will only get worse.

Now you have a clear statement. Note, however, that if the original sentence had been embedded in a paragraph, it would be clear who they refers to:

The world's scientific experts agree. They say that global warming will only get worse.

Context is everything; in this context, *they* has a clear antecedent: the *world's scientific experts.*

Modifiers and Modification

Modifying Words
A **modifier** is a word or a phrase that describes another word or phrase. The most familiar examples are adjectives and adverbs. **Adjectives** describe nouns or pronouns; **adverbs** describe verbs, adjectives, or other adverbs. Here are some examples:

Adjectives

The loud noise shocked us.

The fruitful hypothesis led to interesting experiments.

Adverbs

Al spoke convincingly.

Stephen fought viciously.

A common error is using an adjective when an adverb is required. For example, why is the following sentence incorrect?

I take that remark serious.

Serious is an adjective modifying *take*, which is a verb. That's a no-no; it should be:

I take that remark seriously.

You should also strive to use the proper form of an adjective. Adjectives can take three forms, as you can see in the following chart:

Descriptive	Comparative	Superlative
hot	hotter	hottest
dull	duller	dullest
complex	more complex	most complex
good	better	best
bad	worse	worst

Most adjectives follow the forms exemplified by *hot* and *dull*. Some, like *complex*, require *more* for the **comparative** and *most* for the **superlative.** *Good* and *bad*, and some others, are irregular.

Consider the following sentences:

Of the three cars, that one is cheaper.

That car is cheapest than this one.

Both are incorrect. The comparative form should be used with two objects; the superlative with three or more objects. The sentences should be:

That car is cheaper than this one.

Of the three cars, that one is cheapest.

Modifying Phrases

Phrases can act as modifiers too, and this is where things get a little trickier. Mastering this concept will greatly improve your essay.

Roaring into the Florida sky, the space shuttle awed the spectators.

The phrase *roaring into the Florida sky* is a unit that modifies *the space shuttle.* But what if we wrote the sentence as follows?

Roaring into the Florida sky, the spectators were awed by the space shuttle.

What this second sentence is saying is that *the spectators* were *roaring into the Florida sky.* That would truly be an awe-inspiring sight!

This is the storied **dangling modifier.** The modifier *roaring into the Florida sky* dangles off the front of the sentence, unconnected to *the space shuttle*, the phrase it modifies.

Some other examples of dangling modifiers follow; they can be pretty funny once you recognize the error:

Incorrect: *Smoking a big cigar, the baby was admired by its father.*

Comment: *There's very little chance that any baby would be precocious enough to smoke a cigar.*

Correct: *Smoking a big cigar, the father admired his baby.*

Incorrect: *Playing drums for too long, there is a chance of injury.*

Comment: *This modifier is dangling by a thread—what could playing drums for too long modify in this sentence?*

Correct: *If you play drums for too long, you risk injury.*

Incorrect: *Swearing in frustration, my computer continually crashed as I rushed to complete my paper.*

Comment: *Was the computer doing the swearing? I don't think technology is quite there yet.*

Correct: *Swearing in frustration, I rushed to complete my paper as my computer crashed continually.*

Incorrect: *To write a good essay, a lot of material needs to be mastered.*

Comment: *We're missing the noun that needs modification—who needs to master a lot of material?*

Correct: *To write a good essay, essay-writers need to master a lot of material.*

Another frequent writing error that obscures meaning is the **misplaced modifier.** Here's an example:

The teacher posted the grades for the students earned on the midterm.

In this sentence, the phrase *earned on the midterm* seems to modify the *students*, when it should modify the *grades*. This is confusing; here's a rewrite:

The teacher posted the grades earned on the midterm for the students.

Clause Organization

A **clause** is a group of words that has a subject and a predicate. Sentences can have one clause or many clauses. Clauses are the building blocks of sentences and are very important units of meaning; essentially, they create a logical flow. The position of clauses and phrases and the punctuation used to connect them generates the flow that all good writing must have. Varying your clause structure will help make your essay stand out.

The following sentence has three clauses, each of which is underlined:

Einstein shocked most of his peers when *he proved that measurements of time, length,*
    Clause 1   **Clause 2**

and mass were relative to the observer because *Newtonian physics had assumed these*
       Clause 2   **Clause 3**

measurements to be absolute regardless of the observer.
       Clause 3

The words that are not underlined are the all-important connections between the clauses. They guide the reader from clause to clause. Appropriate connections require that you follow logic as well as grammar. As much as any feature of language, their proper use creates the flow so valued by your readers.

In the sentence above, *when* lets the reader know that what shocked most of Einstein's peers is about to be announced. Furthermore, since *when* is a temporal word, you know that something specific happened at some specific point in time. *Because* lets you know that the reason why his peers were so stunned is about to be revealed.

Logical flow is most obviously transmitted by signpost words, which often link paragraphs. English has many such guide words and phrases. Here's a handy list of some common ones; be sure you can use them properly:

and	consequently	nevertheless	thus
also	despite	no less than	therefore
although	even	or	though
as well as	for	otherwise	yet
because	however	so	
but	moreover	still	

The Weak *And*

One common feature of poor clause connection is the weak *and*. Think about it: what does *and* mean? It's pretty much the word version of the + symbol. *And* denotes addition or the mere presence of two equivalent things at the same time or in the same place:

> Frank likes beans and Mongo likes cheese.

You feel like shrugging your shoulders and saying, "Well, Frank likes his beans; Mongo likes his cheese. To each his own, I guess." *And* doesn't *lead* the reader anywhere. It makes no causal connection. It stops the flow dead in its tracks.

The following sentence has the same problem:

> Darwin's theory of natural selection shocked Victorian England and a pillar of
> Victorian culture had been that a benevolent deity had specially created all species.

Huh? You know that this sentence just cries out for causation; substitute *because* for *and* to make this sentence flow:

> Darwin's theory of natural selection shocked Victorian England because a pillar of
> Victorian culture had been that a benevolent deity had specially created all species.

Comparisons

In this section, we'll explore two other crucial features of clause structure. What's wrong with the following sentence?

> Like England, parliaments have been adopted in other countries.

What exactly is being compared here? *England* and *parliaments* or *England* and *other countries?* Right, *England* and *other countries*. This is a perfect example of how imprecise use of language will obscure your meaning and decrease the effectiveness of your essay.

To fix this, put the two things being compared next to each other:

> Like England, other countries have adopted parliaments.

Also note the passive construction of the first, incorrect sentence. You'll find that these errors compound and entail each other. Luckily, fixing one often leads to fixing others automatically.

Another, trickier, example:

> Like classical economics, Darwin focused on individuals.

It doesn't make sense to *compare classical* economics to *Darwin*. You're comparing an area of study to a person. You must always compare like with like. Here are some ways to fix this problem:

Like classical economics, Darwinian evolution focused on individuals.

Like classical economists, Darwin focused on individuals.

As you strive to vary your sentence structure, watch out for the long intervening clause.

Like classical economics, which is still the reigning orthodoxy, Darwin focused on individuals.

It doesn't matter how long the intervening clause is—this is still incorrect. While it's a good idea to vary your sentence length, be on the lookout for agreement and comparison errors.

Like vs. As

Another key concept is the difference between *like* and *as*. Use *like* to compare **nouns** (persons, places, things, or ideas):

That man looks like Mick Jagger.

Use as to compare **verbs**:

That man sings soulfully, just as Mick Jagger does.

Parallelism

Parallel structure is not only a sign of good writing, but it also serves to vary your sentence structure, carry your argument forward, and clarify your meaning. It's also easy to grasp and use.

First, certain stock phrases have to follow a certain form. Look at this chart:

Form	Example
neither/nor	That cyclist has neither the equipment nor the endurance to attempt a 100-mile ride.
either/or	You can have either a bagel or a donut.

Form	Example
not only/but also	Writing a successful essay requires not only good argumentation but also effective use of language.
the more/the more	The more you eat, the more weight you'll gain.
the less/the less	The less pollution we breathe, the less chance we'll have of becoming ill later in life.
both/and	Both ants and bees cooperate so closely that they could be considered "superorganisms."
if/then	If you want to write a strong essay, then read this book and practice.

These forms should always be maintained: don't write *neither/or* or *not only/but*.

Second, learn to apply parallelism properly. Look at this sentence:

> *I walk a lot, but, on the other hand, I seem to spend a lot of time sitting on the couch.*

You have *the other hand*, but where's the first hand? This sentence is not parallel. To fix it, write:

> *On the one hand, I walk a lot, but on the other hand, I seem to spend a lot of time sitting on the couch.*

What's wrong with the following sentence?

> *Not only do I like to swim, but I also like water-skiing.*

The verb in the first clause is an infinitive, *to swim*. But the verb in the second part is a gerund, *water-skiing*. Fix it in one of two ways:

> *Not only do I like to swim, but I also like to water-ski.*

> *Not only do I like swimming, but I also like water-skiing.*

The need for parallel structure arises in series as well. The following sentence is incorrect:

> *Ethan likes knitting, boxing, and to read.*

Again, you have two ways to fix this:

Ethan likes knitting, boxing, and reading.

Ethan likes to knit, to box, and to read.

Another kind of parallelism mistake is the following:

Composing with a computer is better than when you compose with pen and paper.

To fix this, make sure your verbs are in the same form:

Composing with a computer is better than composing with pen and paper.

As usual, pay special attention to sentences you write that have long intervening clauses:

Composing with a computer, which allows you to hear what you're composing as you work, is better than when you compose with pen and paper.

Change *when you compose* to *composing*, just as we did in the previous incorrect sentence.

Usage

Word Choice

Word choice is a key feature of good essays. The proper and appropriate use of words can really impress. We talked a little about wordiness and the importance of variety earlier in the chapter.

Idioms and Prepositional Idioms

Idioms are inherited quirks of language that we absorb without question but which cause nonnative speakers endless trouble.

For example, here's an idiom we've all used:

It wasn't me.

Look at this grammatically. A pronoun that refers only to humans, *me*, is replacing a pronoun that refers only to inanimate objects, *it*. However, every native English-speaker knows what this phrase means and has probably used it quite effectively.

These types of idioms are so dangerously close to clichés that you should avoid them at all costs.

That said, the proper use of another type of idiom will definitely impress your readers. The particular meaning of certain words requires the use of a particular preposition:

Incorrect: *Helga prefers poetry over novels.*

Correct: *Helga prefers poetry to novels.*

Incorrect: *Barack doesn't have a favorable opinion toward Freud's theories.*

Correct: *Barack doesn't have a favorable opinion of Freud's theories.*

Sometimes, a word can be combined legitimately with more than one preposition, but the meaning will then shift. Knowing which preposition triggers which meaning is crucial to good usage.

My remark was meant as a joke.

You, my friend, are meant for greatness.

Meant as shows intent; *meant for* indicates a destination. A complete and relatively short list of such **prepositional idioms** can also be found in *SparkNotes Ultimate Style* (**www.sparknotes.com/ultimatestyle**).

Double Negatives

Finally, let's consider double negatives. When we want to negate something, we use *no* or *not*:

*I allow **no** talking during a movie.*

*I do **not** allow talking during a movie.*

For reasons of redundancy and idiomatic preference, we don't use both *no* and *not* in the same sentence:

I do not allow no talking during a movie.

Words other than *no* and *not* can indicate negation. A list of those words with their positive counterparts (which are not necessarily their antonyms) is on page 119. Don't use a negative word with *not* or *no*.

Three other words are often involved in double negatives: *hardly, scarcely,* and *barely.*

I can't hardly wait to graduate. (Two negatives—can't and hardly)

Believe it or not, this is not grammatically incorrect. But it has fallen into extreme idiomatic disfavor. Do not use these words in your essay! Instead, use:

I can hardly wait to graduate. (One negative—hardly)

I can't wait to graduate. (One negative—can't).

Negative Word	Positive Counterpart	Examples
never	ever	**Incorrect:** *I don't never eat meat.* **Correct:** *I never eat meat.* **Correct:** *I don't ever eat meat.*
none	any	**Incorrect:** *I don't want none.* **Correct:** *I want none.* **Correct:** *I don't want any.*
neither	either	**Incorrect:** *I don't want neither of those two puppies.* **Correct:** *I want neither of those two puppies.* **Correct:** *I don't want either of those two puppies.*
nor	or	**Incorrect:** *I don't want the puppy nor the kitten.* **Correct:** *I want neither the puppy nor the kitten.* **Correct:** *I don't want the puppy or the kitten.*
nothing	anything	**Incorrect:** *I don't want nothing from you.* **Correct:** *I want nothing from you.* **Correct:** *I don't want anything from you.*
no one	anyone	**Incorrect:** *I can't help no one.* **Correct:** *I can help no one.* **Correct:** *I can't help anyone.*
nobody	anybody	**Incorrect:** *I don't know nobody here.* **Correct:** *I know nobody here.* **Correct:** *I don't know anybody here.*
nowhere	anywhere	**Incorrect:** *I can't go nowhere with this cast on my leg.* **Correct:** *I can go nowhere with this cast on my leg.* **Correct:** *I can't go anywhere with this cast on my leg.*

9

THE FINAL EDIT

"I don't write easily or rapidly. My first draft usually has only a few elements worth keeping. I have to find what those are and build from them and throw out what doesn't work, or what simply is not alive."

Susan Sontag

Now you are about to embark on the last stage in the writing process: the final edit. But before you go any further, close this book, turn off your computer, put down your pencil, and take a break. That's right: relax. Go to a movie with your friends, watch TV, or find a good party to go to. Do anything but look at your essay, and try not to even think about it.

Why? Because when you come back to it, you will be refreshed and in a much better position to look at your essay with a critical eye. Weaknesses that you missed three days ago, new ideas for transitions, tighter sentence constructions, and stronger words will pop out at you.

Be Critical

"There are days when the result is so bad that no fewer than five revisions are required. In contrast, when I'm greatly inspired, only four revisions are needed."

John Kenneth Galbraith

Imagine how a stranger would read your essay. Ask yourself: what works, what needs more work, what's missing, and what can be deleted? Did you say what you set out to say? Are your tone and message consistent throughout?

In the last chapter, we talked about common mechanical errors to watch out for. In this chapter, we'll discuss how to edit for content, and we'll offer some proofreading tips to avoid sloppy oversights.

Some people like to edit on screen, while others find it easier to print out their essays, mark changes in pen, and then go back and input corrections. The only way to know which method works best for you is to try them all and see which feels most natural. If you choose to edit on screen, consider working on it in "print layout" view so you can see what your words will actually look like on the page.

The final editing stage can be exciting. You can feel the power of your words taking shape, your ideas coming together, and your best, most polished voice emerging.

"Hire" an Editor

You may feel you don't need help with your essay because the writing is so subjective. After all, how can someone else tell you what's right or wrong when it's *your* life you are talking about? This kind of reasoning is precisely why it's so important to get help. When you write about something so close to you, it's hard to tell whether it's clear, whether you're explaining too much or not enough, or whether you are conveying your point. Your essay is so much a part of you that it can be hard to see whether it's working. Also you've been working on this for a while, and it's easy to lose perspective.

Even the top writers need another set of eyes to look at their work. It's much easier for someone who didn't write the essay to point out redundancies, inconsistencies, or awkward, vague, and unclear spots in which you need to develop your ideas further and more clearly.

> "Remember, it is no sign of weakness or defeat that your manuscript ends up in need of major surgery. This is common in all writing and among the best of writers."
>
> **E. B. White**

Whom to Ask

Find a trusted friend, relative, or teacher who knows you well and ask for feedback. "Some students think that if it's not perfect the first time it's somehow a reflection on their character," says Margret Korzus, Associate Dean of Admissions at the University of Denver. "You really need to learn to be able to take help."

Make sure to ask your reader, "Does it sound like me?" and have him/her mark places where you sound like you're trying too hard to impress. Have your reader look for grammatical errors, awkwardness, organizational problems, and gaps in your story or logic.

Pick one person to read your essay and give you feedback. If you have too many people giving you advice, you will go crazy. Plus, taking everyone's suggestions into account would dilute your voice. Be sure to ask someone whose judgment you trust and who is likely to tell you the truth, rather than to placate or flatter you.

Build in extra time for your reader to review your essay and give you feedback. Be prepared to nag if she doesn't respond with her comments within the timeframe you requested.

Show Mom or Dad

Should you show your mom or dad? It depends on your parent. If your parents are writers, for example, you might benefit from their insight. But if your topic is sensitive and your parents might not respond well, consider asking a teacher, friend, college counselor, or other relative instead.

Your parents feel fairly invested in your future. They definitely want the best for you and want to see you succeed. In other words, parents are not exactly disinterested parties. They may feel entitled to tell you what to write about and how to represent yourself.

Get Feedback

It's natural to feel defensive about any questions asked or suggestions made about your writing. After all, you've really been pouring your blood, sweat, and tears into the essay. You may feel like your reader just didn't pay close enough attention or is making random and gratuitous suggestions.

For these reasons, it's a good idea to take a break while your reader is reviewing your essay. With a little distance, you are likely to feel less frustrated and defensive when you hear suggestions or corrections.

Try not to take negative feedback personally. You do not need to blindly accept every suggestion you receive, but remind yourself that, ultimately, feedback from a reader will probably make your essay stronger.

Read for Content

After you've read your reader's comments and made revisions, read the essay again. Is what you've written believable? Are your ideas and examples clear? Is the point of your essay clear? Do you make it clear near the beginning so the reader knows why she is reading it? Does every paragraph and sentence develop and support your main point?

Read it through several more times, each time focusing on a different aspect.

Is Your Essay Organized?

We discussed the importance of topic sentences in Chapter 6. Make sure after all the rearranging and editing you've done that your paragraphs still have topic sentences. Try underlining the topic sentences of each paragraph. If you read just the topic sentences they should follow logically and form a mini-essay that makes sense.

Go through your essay paragraph by paragraph. Make sure each sentence refers to the idea stated in your topic sentences. Delete any irrelevant sentences, or move them to a different paragraph. If you're not sure where to put a sentence, create a new document for wayward sentences. Later on, you can figure out where they might work.

How Does Your Essay Sound?

Read your essay aloud. Hearing your words is really helpful in terms of figuring out what works and what doesn't. Close your door, ignore how silly you feel, and listen to how the words sound. This is a trick of the trade that many writers use. It allows you to hear the rhythm of your sentences.

Does your tongue get tied when you read your sentences aloud? Do you need to take a breath in the middle of a sentence? If so, maybe your sentences are too long. Break them into simpler sentences. But also make sure your sentences aren't too short and choppy; combine sentences if need be. Finally, as we discussed in Chapter 8, it is important to mix up the length of your sentences for variety and rhythm.

Do you repeat the same words throughout your essay? See if you can come up with synonyms. Look in a thesaurus for similar words but make sure you actually understand the new word you are using and the way you are using it.

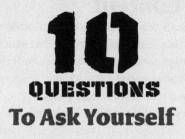

10
QUESTIONS
To Ask Yourself

1

Do I like the sequence of ideas?

2

Are related ideas grouped together?

3

Is my introduction clear and powerful?

4

Is there a logical sequence to my sentences?

5

Does each paragraph present a new idea?

6

Do I use transitions to help the reader follow my thoughts?

7

Have I checked thoroughly for grammatical and spelling errors?

8

Am I telling a good story?

9

Is my vocabulary varied?

10

Does my conclusion tie everything together?

Upgrade Your Verbs

The more specific your verbs, the more powerful and fresh your essay will sound. In Chapter 7, we offered advice on how to choose the best verbs. Instead of writing, *I went to my aunt's house*, think about how you went. Did you walk? If so, how? Did you take the bus?

Instead of relying on adverbs (*I hungrily ate the sandwich*), think of a verb that might more specifically describe the action (*I gobbled the sandwich*). When you have an adjective that *tells*, exchange it for a verb that *shows*. For example, instead of *happy baby*, write *Clara cooed*. Instead of *dangerous dog*, write *the Rottweiler growled and showed its teeth*.

> **Change:** *It got cold out.*
>
> **To:** *The temperature plummeted.*

> **Change:** *The reckless cab driver went down Broadway.*
>
> **To:** *The cab careened down Broadway.*

> **Change:** *Jane happily went to school.*
>
> **To:** *Jane skipped into the classroom with a smile spread across her face.*

Tone and Consistency

As we discussed in Chapter 5, your voice should remain consistent throughout your essay. When you incorporate your reader's comments and suggestions into your draft, make sure you remain true to your voice. You don't want the admissions officer to suddenly come across a section that sounds like someone else wrote it.

Paragraph Length

Look at your essay paragraph by paragraph. Are any of your paragraphs supershort? Is that the case because you haven't fully developed your ideas? Push your ideas further by looking at each sentence and asking yourself, "So what?" Did you take your ideas as far as you could? (We discussed this in detail in Chapter 4.)

MORE QUESTIONS
To Ask Yourself

1

Did I follow the essay directions?

2

Does my tone match the content of my essay?

3

Do I sound like me?

4

Am I trying too hard to impress?

5

Do I orient my reader? (Will my reader be able to tell where s/he is when I start my story and where the essay is going/what the point is?)

6

Are my references to history, literature, math, science, or politics, if any, accurate?

7

Is my writing too wordy?

8

Do I make generalizations?

9

Do I overstate or exaggerate?

10

Have I left out any words by mistake?

Are any of your paragraphs too long? Are you repeating yourself? Can you cut any irrelevant sentences? If you've already cut out all irrelevant sentences and made sure you're not repeating yourself, consider breaking your paragraph into two (or more) shorter paragraphs. Big, dense chunks of text are not inviting for the reader.

Special Warning:
Make Sure You Have the Right College Name

Most admissions officers say their #1 pet peeve is when an applicant puts the wrong college name in the essay.

"I would say that out of the 6,551 applications we got this year, maybe 200 had something along the lines of: 'And that is why I'm so eager to be a part of the first-year class next year at College X,'" writes Gary Ross, Dean of Admissions at Colgate University. "The only problem is that College X isn't Colgate."

10

REAL ESSAYS

"To read a writer is for me not merely to get an idea of what he says, but to go off with him and travel in his company."

André Gide

The best way to improve your writing is to read good writing. You are already doing that in your English class; we also gave you a list of notable memoirs by celebrated authors in Chapter 2. Here, we've compiled some sample essays from people who have recently completed the college application process. These essays were chosen for their clarity, originality, voice, and style.

As you can see, some are emotional, some are cerebral, and some are a combination of the two. Others are funny, serious, philosophical, and creative. They are as different as the personalities of the people who wrote them, but what these essays all have in common is their honesty and the effort the writers put into creating them.

These personal statements have one other thing in common: *the authors were admitted to the colleges of their choice.*

Allison Dencker
Stanford University, Class of 2006

As you reflect on life thus far, what has someone said, written, or expressed in some fashion that is especially meaningful to you. Why?

According to Mother Teresa, "If you judge someone, you have no time to love them." I first saw this quote when it was posted on my sixth-grade classroom wall, and I hated it. Rather, I hated Mother Teresa's intention, but I knew that the quote's veracity was inarguable. I felt that it was better to judge people so as not to have to love them, because some people don't deserve a chance. Judgments are shields, and mine was impenetrable.

Laura was my dad's first girlfriend after my parents' divorce. The first three years of our relationship were characterized solely by my hatred toward her, manifested in my hurting her, each moment hurting myself twice as much. From the moment I laid eyes on her, she was the object of my unabated hatred, not because of anything she had ever done, but because of everything she represented. I judged her to be a heartless, soulless, two-dimensional figure: she was a representation of my loneliness and pain. I left whenever she entered a room, I slammed car doors in her face. Over those three years, I took pride in the fact that I had not spoken a word to her or made eye contact with her. I treated Laura with such resentment and anger because my hate was my protection, my shield. I, accustomed to viewing her as the embodiment of my pain, was afraid to let go of the anger and hate, afraid to love the person who allowed me to hold onto my anger, afraid that if I gave her a chance, I might love her.

For those three years, Laura didn't hate me; she understood me. She understood my anger and my confusion, and Laura put her faith in me, although she had every reason not to. To her, I was essentially a good person, just confused and scared; trying to do her best, but just not able to get a hold of herself. She saw me as I wished I could see myself.

None of this became clear to me overnight. Instead, over the next two years, the one-dimensional image of her in my mind began to take the shape of a person. As I let go of my hatred, I gave her a chance. She became a woman who, like me, loves *Ally McBeal* and drinks a lot of coffee; who, unlike me, buys things advertised on infomercials.

Three weeks ago, I saw that same Mother Teresa quote again, but this time I smiled. Laura never gave up on me, and the chance she gave me to like her was a chance that changed my life. Because of this, I know the value of a chance, of having faith in a person, of seeing others as they wish they could see themselves. I'm glad I have a lot of time left, because I definitely have a lot of chances left to give, a lot of people left to love.

Jeremy Chapman
Duke University, Class of 2005

Topic of your choice.

Me(s): A One-Act Play

(*Several of me occupy themselves around my bedroom. Logical me sits attentively in my desk chair. Lighthearted me hangs upside-down, off the back of my recliner. Existentialist me leans against my door, eyebrows raised. Stressed me, Independent me, and Artistic me are also present.*)

Stressed: So, come on, what's this meeting about?

Logical: (*Taking a deep breath*) Well, it's time we come together. It's time we create "Jeremy."

Lighthearted: (*Furrowing his brow, but smiling*) What? Is this "Captain Planet," where all the characters join fists and out bursts the superhero?

Logical: No, this meeting is an opportunity to evaluate where we are in life, like a State of the Union Address.

Existentialist: Speaking of which, I've been meaning to ask all of you: college? Honestly, is it worth it? You . . . *(gestures toward Logical)* you're writing that philosophy book, which should do well. And look at Artsy over there! He's composing music, making beautiful art; why don't we see where we can get with that? Not to mention the endless possibilities if Lighthearted aims for *Saturday Night Live*. Think about the number of successful people in this world who didn't go to college! *(Logical shakes his head)* I mean, let's be realistic: if we go to college, eventually we'll be required to declare a major. Once we earn a degree, it might be harder to pursue our true passions—comedy, music, art . . .

Logical: Not true. First of all, you failed to mention *my* fascinations with neurology and psychology, which are potential majors at every university. Furthermore, opportunities to study comedy, music, and art are available at all colleges too; we just have to go after them. *(Sends a reassuring nod toward Artistic)* In fact, if anything, college will facilitate our involvement in activities like drawing, improvisational comedy, piano, psychological experiments, Japanese, ping-pong . . .

Artistic: Yeah—imagine how much better I'd be at writing music if I took a music-composition course.

Logical: Exactly. And what about our other educational goals such as becoming fluent in Japanese, learning the use of every TI-89 calculator button . . .

Independent: I agree. Plus, I was thinking of college as a social clean slate. I am looking forward to living on my own—away from our overprotective, over-scrutinizing family. No more hesitating to ask girls out!

Lighthearted: *(He has not been paying attention to the discussion)* What ever *happened* to Captain Planet? He was like, really popular in 1987 and then . . .

Stressed: Enough out of you. *(Lighthearted makes a mocking face at Stressed)* You're giving me a headache. By the way, everyone, we're not making much progress here, and I'm beginning to feel a stress-pimple coming on. *(All except Existential gather around Stressed and comfort him)*

Existential: There's really no reason to be stressed about anything. If you think about how trivial—how meaningless—all this worry is, it's kind of pathetic that your anxiety is about to get us all stuck with a pimple.

Independent: I don't know what you're talking about, Mr. I-Know-Everything-And-It-All-Means-Nothing, but mightn't we as well calm down Stressed?

Existential: If you consider that your top priority right now. I thought we came here to do something else.

Stressed: He's right, I'm fine. Let's just get back to work, and the problem will heal itself. Where were we?

Lighthearted: We were searching through the late 80s for Captain Planet's mysterious disapp . . . *(Stressed plugs his ears and momentarily steps out of the room; Independent shoves Lighthearted; Logic buries his face in his hands; Artistic begins doodling; Existential laughs)*

Existential: We're a bunch of fools. It amazes me that we all squeezed into the same person. You know, if you think about the conversation we just had, it *does* reveal a lot about "Jeremy."

Artistic: *(Chewing his pencil)* He's got a point. And I thought of a cool song. So we were productive, after all. We should congregate like this more often. We can go places if we stick together.

All: Yeah, we can. *(They all put their right fists together, and there is a sudden burst of light and thunderous sound, as in the old "Captain Planet" cartoons, followed by a knocking on the door)*

Parents: Jeremy, are you OK? What's all that noise?

Jeremy: Yeah, I'm fine. Just puttin' myself together. I think I've got a good idea for a college application essay . . .

Soraya Palmer
Connecticut College, Class of 2007

Evaluate a significant experience, achievement, risk you have taken, or ethical dilemma you have faced and its impact on you.

Finding Truths

In my life, I have taken many journeys without which I would not have experienced important truths. My father started us off early, taking us on many journeys to help us understand that true knowledge comes only from experience. We took trips every winter break to Madrid, Mexico, Costa Rica, and to Jamaica and Trinidad, my parents' homeland for Christmas. Silly things I remember from those trips include the mango chili sauce on the pork in Maui, the names of the women who gave out the towels by the pools in Selva Verde, Costa Rica, eating dinner at 10 P.M. in Spain. These were all tourist experiences that I, at first, found spellbinding. My truths were the truths of the tourist brochures: beautiful hotels, beaches, and cities. I did not see the blindfolds. I did not appreciate how being held hostage by the beauty of the surface—the beaches and cities—blinded me to the absence of Puerto Rican natives on the streets of San Juan; I did not understand how the prevalence and familiarity of English conspired to veil the beauty of the Spanish language beneath volumes of English translations.

I learned more about these truths in my sophomore year of high school, when I was among a group of students selected to visit Cuba. My grandmother was born in Cuba, yet I had never thought to research my own heritage. I have remained the naïve American who saw Castro as some distant enemy of my country, accepting this as fact because this seemed to be the accepted wisdom. I soon became intrigued, however, with this supposed plague to my freedom, my culture, and everything good and decent. I began to think, just what is communism anyway? What's so bad about Castro and Cuba—and I hear they have good coffee. I believed that what was missing was a lack of understanding between our two cultures, and that acceptance of our differences would come only with knowledge.

My first impression of Cuba was the absence of commercialism. I saw no giant golden arch enticing hungry Cubans with beef-laced fries; I did see billboards of Che Guevara and signposts exhorting unity and love. I realized, however, that much of the uniqueness that I relished here might be gone if the trade blockades in Cuba were ever lifted. The parallels and the irony were not lost on me. I was stepping out of an American political cave that shrouded the beauty of Cuba and stepping into another, one built on patriotic socialism, one where truths were just as ideological as, yet very different from, mine.

History, I recognized, is never objective. The journeys I have taken have been colored by my prior experiences and by what my feelings were in those moments. Everyone holds a piece of the truth. Maybe facts don't matter. Perhaps my experience is my truth and the more truths I hear from everyone else, the closer I will get to harmonization. Maybe there is no harmony, and I must go through life challenging and being challenged, perhaps finding perspectives from which I can extract—but never call— truth. I must simply find ways to understand others, to seek in them what is common to us all and perhaps someday find unity in our common human bond. This is what life has taught me so far, my sum of truths gleaned from experiencing many cultures. I don't know if these truths will hold, but I hope that my college experience will be like my trip to Cuba—challenging some truths, strengthening others, and helping me experience new ones.

Daniele Melia
New York University, Class of 2007

A range of academic interests, personal perspectives, and life experiences adds much to the educational mix. Given your personal background, describe an experience that illustrates what you would bring to the diversity in the college community or an encounter that demonstrated the importance of diversity to you.

I feel sick. I'm nervous and my stomach's turning. The room is lined with neat rows of desks, each one occupied by another kid my age. We're all about to take the SATs. The proctor has instructed us to fill out section four: "race."

I cannot be placed neatly into a single racial category, although I'm sure that people walking down the street don't hesitate to label me "caucasian." Never in my life has a stranger not been surprised when I told them I was half black.

Having light skin, eyes, and hair, but being black *and* white often leaves me misperceived. Do I wish that my skin were darker so that when I tell people I'm black they won't laugh at me? No, I accept and value who I am. To me, being black is more than having brown skin; it's having ancestors who were enslaved, a grandfather who managed one of the nation's oldest black newspapers, the *Chicago Daily Defender,* and a family who is as proud of their heritage as I am. I prove that one cannot always discern another's race by his or her appearance.

I often find myself frustrated when explaining my racial background, because I am almost always proving my "blackness" and left neglecting my Irish-American side. People have told me that "one drop of black blood determines your race," but I opt not to follow this rule. In this country a century ago, most mixed-race children were products of rape or other relationships of power imbalance, but I am not. I am a child in the twenty-first century who is a product of a loving relationship. I choose the label *biracial* and identify with my black and Irish sides equally. I am proud to say that my paternal great-grandparents immigrated to this country from Ireland and that I have found their names on the wall at Ellis Island, but people are rarely interested in that. They can't get over the idea that this girl, who according to their definition looks white, is not.

Last year, at my school's "Sexual Awareness Day," a guest lecturer spoke about the stereotypical portrayal of different types of people on MTV's *The Real World*. He pointed out that the white, blond-haired girls are always depicted as completely ditsy and asked me how it felt to fit that description. I wasn't surprised that he assumed I was white, but I did correct his mistake. I told him that I thought the show's portrayal of white girls with blond hair was unfair. I went on to say that we should also be careful not to make assumptions about people based on their physical appearance. "For example," I told him, "I'm not white." It was interesting that the lecturer, whose goal was to teach students not to judge or make assumptions about people based on their sexual orientation, had himself made a racial assumption about me.

I often find myself wishing that racial labels didn't exist so that people wouldn't rely on race alone to understand a person's thoughts, actions, habits, and personality. One's race does not reveal the content of their character. When someone finds out that I am biracial, do I become a different person in his or her eyes? Am I suddenly "deeper," because I'm not just the "plain white girl" they assumed I was? Am I more complex? Can they suddenly relate to me more (or less)? No, my race alone doesn't reveal who I am. If one's race cannot be determined simply by looking at a person, then how can it be possible to look at a person and determine her inner qualities?

Through census forms, racial questionnaires on the SATs, and other devices, our society tries to draw conclusions about people based on appearance. It is a quick and easy way to categorize people without taking the time to get to know them, but it simply cannot be done.

Ted Mullin
Carleton College, Class of 2006

If you could have lunch with any person, living, dead, or fictional, who would it be and what would you discuss?

We met for lunch at El Burrito Mexicano, a tiny Mexican lunch counter under the Red Line "El" tracks. I arrived first and took a seat, facing the door. Behind me the TV showed highlights from the Mexican Soccer League. I felt nervous and unsure. How would I be received by a famous revolutionary—an upper-middle-class American kid asking a communist hero questions? Then I spotted him in the doorway and my breath caught in my throat. In his overcoat, beard, and beret he looked as if he had just stepped out from one of Batista's "wanted" posters. I rose to greet Ernesto "Che" Guevara and we shook hands. At the counter we ordered: he, enchiladas verdes and a beer, and I, a burrito and two "limonadas." The food arrived and we began to talk.

I told him that I felt honored to meet him and that I admired him greatly for his approach to life. He saw the plight of Latin America's poor and tried to improve their state but went about it on his own terms, not on society's. He waved away my praise with his food-laden fork, responding that he was happy to be here and that it was nice to get out once in a while. Our conversation moved on to his youth and the early choices that set him on his path to becoming a revolutionary.

I have always been curious about what drove Che Guevara to abandon his medical career and take military action to improve the lot of Cuba's poor. Why did he feel that he could do more for the poor as a guerilla leader than as a doctor? His answer was concise: as he came of age he began to realize that the political situation in Latin America had become unacceptable and had to be changed as soon as possible. He saw in many nations "tin-pot" dictators reliant on the United States for economic and military aid, ruining their nations and destroying the lives of their people. He felt morally obligated to change this situation and believed he could help more people in a more direct manner as a warrior rather than as a doctor. Next I asked why he chose communism as the means of achieving his goals.

He replied that communism was merely a means to an end. That end was a Central and South America run by its citizens, free of foreign intervention. In his opinion communism was the best way to realize this dream. I agreed that a nation should be run by and for its citizens, but I hesitated to agree wholeheartedly. I was concerned by his exclusive emphasis on Latin Americans. His description, as I interpreted it, implied a nationalism and exclusion of others, most notably Americans. I felt that this focus on "Latin Americanism" could easily lead to the outbreak of war in the region.

Moving from Cuba's past to its present, I asked him if he sees the revolution begun in 1959 as successful. Has Cuba fulfilled his vision for it? Che Guevara sighed and gathered his thoughts for a moment. Then, speaking slowly, he said that he didn't think that Cuba had fulfilled the revolution because the revolution never spread beyond Cuba, as he had hoped it would. The revolution did not spread, he reasoned, because of the success of the United States in propping up corrupt dictators and the inability of Cuba to build a viable economy upon which to support the export of revolution. I countered his negative view, pointing out that today many of the Latin American countries once under totalitarian rule are democratic, partly due to the spirit of reform he exemplified nearly half a century before. He acknowledged the progress made but remained adamant that the nations were still not free of foreign intervention.

At this point one of the Mexican teams on TV scored a goal, and we broke off our political conversation to talk about soccer. Though I know about European soccer, I know next to nothing about the South American game. He enlightened me, although he admitted his information was a bit out of date. I asked him if he had seen the great Argentinean striker Alfredo Di Stefano play, but Che Guevara said he couldn't remember.

In light of the events of September 11th, I asked about violence. In his view, when is it justified? Che Guevara responded by saying that violence is justified because those who hold power unjustly respond only to violence as a tool for change. They will not willingly relinquish power unless shown that the people will overwhelm and destroy them. I disagreed vociferously, citing Peru and Guatemala as places where violence had been used and failed, only further impoverishing the nations. Che Guevara explained these failures as the inevitable outcome of the revolutionaries losing sight of their original moral goals. Reflecting upon his answers so far, I realized that I had lost some of my admiration for him. By taking up the standard of Pan-American unity, I felt he lost some of his humanity that led me to identify so closely with him. To me he had become more of a symbol than an actual person.

At this point I realized that I had to be home soon and thanked him profusely for his generosity in answering my questions. As we walked toward the door, I noticed that I had left my hat on the table. I turned back to retrieve it, but by the time I had reached the doorway again, Che Guevara had disappeared into the mix of the afternoon sunlight and shadow cast by the "El" tracks, as mysteriously as he had come.

Emily Fiffer
Washington University, Class of 2004

Topic of your choice.

Psst! I have a confession to make. I have a shoe fetish. Everyone around me seems to underestimate the statement a simple pair of shoes can make. To me, though, the shoes I wear are not merely covering for the two feet on which I tread, but a reflection of who I am.

So, who am I? Why don't you look down at my feet? I could be wearing my high-platform sandals—my confidence, my leadership, my I-want-to-be-tall-even-though-I'm-not shoes. My toes are free in these sandals and wiggle at will. Much like my feet in my sandals, I don't like being restricted. I have boundless energy that must not go to waste! Or maybe I'm wearing my furry pink pig slippers. I wear these on crisp winter nights when I'm home spending time with my family. My slippers are my comforting side. I can wear them and listen to a friend cry for hours on end. My favorite pair of shoes, however, are my bright red Dr. Martens. They're my individuality, my enthusiasm, my laughter, my love of risk-taking. No one else I know has them. When I don't feel like drawing attention to my feet or, for that matter, to myself, I wear my gym shoes. These sneakers render me indistinguishable from others and thereby allow me to be independent. I wear them running, riding my bicycle alone through the trails surrounded by signs of autumn, and even when I go to a museum and stand, transfixed by a single photograph. My hiking boots typify my love of adventure and being outdoors. Broken in and molded to the shape of my foot, when wearing them I feel in touch with my surroundings.

During college I intend to add to my collection yet another closet full of colorful clodhoppers. For each aspect of my personality I discover or enhance through my college experiences, I will find a pair of shoes to reflect it. Perhaps a pair of Naot sandals for my Jewish Studies class or one black shoe and one white when learning about the Chinese culture and its belief in yin and yang. As I get to know myself and my goals grow nearer, my collection will expand.

By the time I'm through with college, I will be ready to take a big step. Ready for a change, I believe I'll need only one pair after this point. The shoes will be both fun and comfortable; I'll be able to wear them when I am at work and when I return home. A combination of every shoe in my collection, these shoes will embody each aspect of my personality in a single footstep. No longer will I have a separate pair for each quirk and quality. This one pair will say it all. It will be evidence of my self-awareness and maturity. Sure, I'll keep a few favorites for old times' sake. I'll lace up the old red shoes when I'm feeling rambunctious, when I feel that familiar, teenage surge of energy and remember the girl who wore them: a young girl with the potential to grow.

I am entering college a naïve, teenage bundle of energy, independence, and motivation. My closet full of shoes mirrors my array of interests, and at the same time my difficulty in choosing a single interest that will satisfy me for the rest of my life. I want to leave college with direction, having pinpointed a single interest to pursue that will add texture and meaning to my life.

So there you have it. I've told you about who I am, what I enjoy, and what I want from college. Want to know more? Come walk a day in my shoes.

Leigh Rosen
University of Pennsylvania, Class of 2009

Describe a challenge you overcame.

The stiff black apron hung awkwardly on my hips as I casually tried to tie the strings around my waist. I had been at Gino's Restaurant for only ten minutes when Maurizio, the manager, grabbed my arm abruptly and said, "Follow me to the dungeon." Unsure of whether or not he was joking, I smiled eagerly at him, but his glare confirmed his intent. I wiped the smirk off my face and followed him through the kitchen, which was louder than Madison Square Garden during a Knicks/Pacers game. A tall woman with a thick Italian accent pushed me while barking, "Move it, kid, you're blocking traffic." I later learned she was a waitress, and waitresses did not associate with the low-level busboys. Maurizio brought me to a dangerously steep staircase that looked like it had been purposely drenched in oil to increase the chance of a fall. As he gracefully flew down each step, I clutched onto the rusty tile walls, strategically putting one foot first and then the other. Eventually, I entered the "dungeon" and was directed to a table to join two men who were vigorously folding napkins.

Pretending to know what had to be done, I took a pile of unfolded starched napkins and attempted to turn them into the Gino accordion. I slowly folded each corner, trying to leave exactly one inch on both sides, and ignored the giggles and whispers coming from across the table. When I finished my first napkin, I quickly grabbed another and tried again, hiding my pathetic initial attempt under my thigh. On my second try, I sighed with relief when I saw that what I had constructed slightly resembled an accordion shape. However, when I looked up, I saw that the other two men had each finished twenty perfect napkins. "Hurry up, little girl," they said in unison, "We have lots left." They pointed to a closet overflowing with white linens as I began to fold my third. The next couple of nights afforded me the opportunity to master such tasks as refilling toilet paper dispensers and filling breadbaskets. Just as I began to find solace in these more manageable jobs, I felt a forceful tap on my shoulder. A heavyset waiter who was sweating profusely barked, "I need one decaf cappuccino. Understand?"

"Um, okay," I stuttered, unable to get up enough courage to admit that I had never attempted to make a cappuccino. I glanced over at the intimidating espresso machine and started to pace back and forth. The waiter reappeared and with a look of irritation snapped, "If you didn't know how to do it, why didn't you say so? I don't have time for this!" Returning to the unnecessary re-cleaning of silverware, the only job I could comfortably perform, it dawned on me that my fear of showing ignorance had rendered me incompetent. I had mastered the art of avoidance and had learned nothing. I continued to clean vigorously, making sure to keep my eyes on the silverware so that no one would ask me to make another cappuccino.

Having barely made it through my first weekend at the restaurant, I was amazed at how relieved I felt to return to the familiarity of physics class. We were starting a new chapter on fiber optics. Moving through the material with greater ease than I had anticipated, we hit upon the topic of optical time domain reflectometers, and sweat began to form on my chest as I frantically flipped through my notebook. I marked my paper with an asterisk so that I would know to ask my teacher to explain this material when I met with him privately during my next free period. My teacher then said, "So, I'm sure you all understand OTDR, so let's move on." As all of my peers nodded in agreement, I suddenly realized that I was still not asking how to make cappuccino. I took a deep breath and the fear of not learning overcame my usual fear of looking foolish and I raised my hand. After my question had been answered, I felt like the Red Sox lifting the curse. I erased the star I had made on my notebook and confidently listened as we moved on to the next topic.

I'm not suggesting that raising my hand and asking a question in physics class was a life-changing moment. It did not suddenly rid me of my fear of showing ignorance, but it definitely marked a new willingness to ask questions. When I returned to Gino's the next weekend, I continued to spend some time unnecessarily cleaning silverware, but after asking Maurizio how to use the espresso machine, I soon added making cappuccino to my list of life skills.

PRACTICE
ESSAY
PROMPTS

10 Practice Essay Prompts

To get the writing process started, read the 10 practice prompts below and brainstorm or write a rough draft in the space provided.

1. Discuss a personal achievement that has had a significant impact on your life.

2. Evaluate the pros and cons of a political issue and how it relates to your community.

_____

_____

_____

_____

_____

_____

_____

_____

_____

_____

_____

_____

_____

_____

_____

_____

_____

_____

_____

_____

_____

_____

_____

_____

_____

3. Write an essay describing a person who has influenced you.

4. Write about your favorite book, poem, or play and how it influenced your outlook on the world.

_____

_____

_____

_____

_____

_____

_____

_____

_____

_____

_____

_____

_____

_____

_____

_____

_____

_____

_____

_____

_____

_____

_____

_____

_____

_____

_____

_____

5. The admissions committee has a copy of your autobiography opened to page 367. What does it say?

_____

_____

_____

_____

_____

_____

_____

_____

_____

_____

_____

_____

_____

_____

_____

_____

_____

_____

_____

_____

_____

_____

_____

_____

_____

_____

6. Discuss a challenge you overcame and how it changed you.

7. What is the best advice you have received and why?

_____

_____

_____

_____

_____

_____

_____

_____

_____

_____

_____

_____

_____

_____

_____

_____

_____

_____

_____

_____

_____

_____

_____

_____

_____

_____

_____

8. If you could travel through time, what period in history would you visit and why?

_____

_____

_____

_____

_____

_____

_____

_____

_____

_____

_____

_____

_____

_____

_____

_____

_____

_____

_____

_____

_____

_____

_____

_____

9. You have been selected to meet with the president of the United States for one hour. What would you discuss?

10. If you could switch bodies with one other person for a day, whom would you choose?

ACKNOWLEDGMENTS

First, many thanks to all the college admissions professionals who generously gave their time and insights to help with this book: Meghan Cadwallader of Susquehanna University, Tim Cheney of Connecticut College, Richard DiFeliciantonio of Ursinus College, Eric Furda of Columbia University, Patricia Goldsmith of Scripps College, Francis "Spike" Gummere of Lake Forest College, Margret Korzus of University of Denver, Carol Lunkenheimer of Northwestern, Gary Ross of Colgate University, and Brad Ward of Bucknell University. Also special thanks to Ed Wilson, who, with more than four decades of involvement with the admissions process (at Kellogg School of Management, Northwestern University, New York University's Stern Graduate School of Business, Columbia University, and Bates College) gave me an excellent jumping-off point from which to dive into my research.

Also, I am enormously grateful to the high school English teachers and college counselors who provided me with direction, helped put me in touch with former students, and inspired me with their enthusiasm and extraordinary skill for helping students to craft the best possible essays they can: Alex Darrow, Nancy Lester Elitzer, Krista Klein, Tom Sullivan, Kelly Tanabe, and Betty Weinberger.

And, of course, I would like to recognize and thank the bright students and recent graduates who contributed their essays to the book: Laura Barrow, Jeremy Chapman, Allison Dencker, Emily Fiffer, Daniele Melia, Ted Mullin, Jason O'Bryan, Soraya Palmer, Mike Pomerantz, and Leigh Rosen.

Thanks are due to my editor, Ziki Dekel, for being so sharp, organized, and easygoing all at once. And I couldn't have completed (or even started) this book without the direct and indirect help of many friends and family members. I am also indebted to those of you who contributed to my sanity while I worked on the project, especially when my hard drive crashed and burned midway through the book. You know who you are.

ALSO AVAILABLE
FROM
SPARKCOLLEGE

10 Things You Gotta Know About Choosing a College
ISBN: 1411403509

10 Things You Gotta Know About Paying for College
ISBN: 1411403517

10 Things You Gotta Know About Your First Year of College
ISBN: 1411403525

Visit WWW.SPARKCOLLEGE.COM **for even more stuff you gotta know about colleg**

SPARK
COLLEGE